SUPERPOWERS AT SEA:
AN ASSESSMENT OF THE NAVAL ARMS RACE

STRATEGIC ISSUE PAPERS

SIPRI's new series *Strategic Issue Papers* focuses on topical issues of significance for the future of international peace and security. The naval arms race is quickly emerging as one of the central security and arms control issues of our time. SIPRI has therefore chosen *Superpowers at Sea: An Assessment of the Naval Arms Race* as the second in the series. Further studies in this series will address problems relating to arms reduction, the spread of arms, military and political strategy, and the impact of technology on the conduct of peaceful East-West relations. The books will be concise, with short production times so as to make a timely input into the current debates.

sipri

Stockholm International Peace Research Institute

Sipri is an independent international institute for research into problems of peace and conflict, especially those of arms control and disarmament. It was established in 1966 to commemorate Sweden's 150 years of unbroken peace.

The Institute is mainly financed by the Swedish Parliament. The staff, the Governing Board and the Scientific Council are international.

The Governing Board and the Scientific Council are not responsible for the views expressed in the publications of the Institute.

sipri

Stockholm International Peace Research Institute

Pipers väg 28, S-171 73 Solna, Sweden
Cable: PEACERESEARCH
Telephone: 46 8/55 97 00

Superpowers at Sea: An Assessment of the Naval Arms Race

Richard Fieldhouse
and
Shunji Taoka

Stockholm International Peace Research Institute

Oxford
OXFORD UNIVERSITY PRESS
1989

Oxford University Press, Walton Street, Oxford OX2 6DP
Oxford New York Toronto
Delhi Bombay Calcutta Madras Karachi
Petaling Jaya Singapore Hong Kong Tokyo
Nairobi Dar es Salaam Cape Town
Melbourne Auckland
and associated companies in
Berlin Ibadan

Oxford is a trade mark of Oxford University Press

Published in the United States
by Oxford University Press, New York

© SIPRI 1989

British Library Cataloguing in Publication Data
Fieldhouse, Richard W.
Superpowers at sea: an assessment of the naval arms race.
1. Military equipment: Weapons. Proliferation
I. Title   II. Shuryi, Taska
355.8'2
ISBN 0–19–829135–3

Library of Congress Cataloging in Publication Data
Fieldhouse, Richard W.
Superpowers at sea: an assessment of the naval arms race/
Richard Fieldhouse and Shunji Taoka.   —(Strategic issue papers)
'SIPRI, Stockholm International Peace Research Institute.'
Bibliography   Includes index.
1. Navies—History—20th century.   2. Arms race—History—20th
century.   I. Taoka, Shunji, 1941– .   II. Stockholm International
Peace Research Institute.   III. Title.   IV. Series.
VA40.F54   1989   359'.009'04—dc19   89–2977
ISBN 0–19–829135–3

Printed and bound in
Great Britain by Biddles Ltd,
Guildford and King's Lynn

Preface

Superpowers at Sea is a much needed assessment of the two major navies. It provides the information and understanding of naval forces necessary for a rational debate on this topic. If naval forces and activities are ever to be included in the process of arms control and co-operative security efforts, it is essential that people understand the fundamental facts and realities of the superpower naval competition—from the need for naval forces to the needless dangers they pose. Without such an understanding, all talk of naval arms control—no matter how reasonable—is unlikely to make any progress. As such, *Superpowers at Sea* is a vital contribution to the public understanding of and debate on naval forces and their relationship to arms control and security.

Superpowers at Sea is the first of two publications to result from the SIPRI Project on Naval Forces and Arms Control. The Swedish Government generously gave SIPRI a substantial grant to support the project. In October 1987, SIPRI sponsored an international conference on arms control and naval forces. Many of the papers presented at the conference will appear in the second volume, *Security at Sea: Naval Forces and Arms Control*. This second book begins where *Superpowers at Sea* ends, with a serious consideration of the possibilities and difficulties of naval arms control. Together, the two books constitute a timely and valuable addition to the field.

We at SIPRI were privileged and honoured to have Shunji Taoka join us for one year from the *Asahi Shimbun*, one of Japan's leading newspapers. Taoka, who served in Tokyo as the Senior Staff Correspondent on Military Affairs, brought his wealth of knowledge and experience in naval affairs to SIPRI and has written a superb piece comparing the major navies of East and West. He is now a Senior Editor of *Asahi Shimbun*'s new weekly magazine, *AERA—Asahi Shimbun Extra Report and Analysis*. Richard Fieldhouse, a SIPRI Research Fellow and leader of the Project on Naval Forces and Arms Control, has provided a disturbing exposé and analysis of the nuclearization of the superpower navies. He concludes the monograph with a look towards the future possibilities of naval arms control, the topic of the subsequent book which he is editing.

The authors set out to correct some of the myths and to describe the most important trends and realities of the superpower naval arms race. As the topic of naval forces and arms control gains international and public interest, it is hoped that a constructive and useful debate will emerge.

SIPRI
October 1988

Dr Walther Stützle
Director

Acknowledgements

The authors would like to acknowledge the assistance of several people in the preparation of this monograph. Barbara Adams did a splendid job of editing the monograph, from draft texts to the final product, all with much humour and energy. Åsa Pihlstrand prepared the tables and the final typescripts and, with Gillian Stanbridge's generous and expert help, set the entire monograph in camera-ready format. Cynthia Loo typed the initial drafts of Shunji Taoka's text. Matthew Yeo and Ian Thomas provided assistance with research and acquisition of materials for the monograph, as did the SIPRI Library staff. We extend our gratitude to them all.

Contents

Introduction and overview

Superpowers at Sea: the need for a new assessment
Richard Fieldhouse

Part I. Comparing the navies of East and West

Chapter 1. The superpower naval buildup: a brief history
Shunji Taoka

Chapter 2. East-West naval force comparison
Shunji Taoka

Part II. The naval nuclear arms race

Chapter 3. Naval nuclear weapons: status and implications
Richard Fieldhouse

Part III. Towards naval arms control

Chapter 4. Naval forces and arms control: a look to the future

Richard Fieldhouse

Selected bibliography

Glossary

Abbreviations, acronyms and definitions

AAM	Air-to-air missile
AAW	Anti-air warfare
ABM	Anti-ballistic missile
AEGIS	an advanced air defence system
AEW	Airborne early warning
ALCM	Air-launched cruise missile
ASCM	Anti-ship cruise missile
ASM	Air-to-surface missile
ASMP	Air-Sol-Moyenne-Portée (France)
ASROC	Anti-*s*ubmarine *roc*ket
ASTOR	Anti-*s*ubmarine *tor*pedo
ASUW	Anti-surface warfare
ASW	Anti-submarine warfare
ASW/SOW	Anti-submarine warfare stand-off weapon
BMD	Ballistic missile defence
C^3I	Command, control, communications and intelligence
CAPTOR	En*cap*sulated *tor*pedo
CBM	Confidence-building measures
CDE	Conference on Disarmament in Europe
CLS	Capsule Launch System
CO	Commanding Officer
CTOL	Conventional take-off and landing
CZ	Convergence zone
DoD	Department of Defense (US)
ELF	Extremely low frequency
FEBA	Forward edge of battle area
FOST	Force Océanique Stratégique (France)
FRAS	Free rocket anti-submarine
GIUK	Greenland-Iceland-UK
GLCM	Ground-launched cruise missile
HF	High frequency
HQ	Headquarters
ICBM	Intercontinental ballistic missile

INF	Intermediate-range nuclear forces
JCS	Joint Chiefs of Staff (US)
kt	kiloton
MIRV	Multiple independently targetable re-entry vehicle
Mod	modification
MRV	Multiple re-entry vehicle
Mt	megaton
NATO	North Atlantic Treaty Organization
NG	Nouvelle generation (France)
NST	Nuclear and Space Talks
OTH	Over the horizon
PAL	Permissive Action Link
PVO	Air defence force (Soviet)
SALT	Strategic Arms Limitation Talks
SAM	Surface-to-air missile
SDI	Strategic Defense Initiative
shp	shaft horsepower
SIOP	Single Integrated Operational Plan
SLBM	Submarine-launched ballistic missile
SLCM	Sea-launched cruise missile
SNA	Soviet Naval Aviation
SOSUS	*So*und *su*rveillance *s*ystem
START	Strategic Arms Reduction Talks
SUBROC	*Sub*marine *roc*ket
TNF	Theatre nuclear forces
V/STOL	Vertical/short take-off and landing
VLA	Vertical Launch ASROC
VLF	Very low frequency
VLS	Vertical Launch System
VTOL	Vertical take-off and landing
WTO	Warsaw Treaty Organization

Ship designations

BB	Battleship
CG	Guided missile-equipped cruiser
CGN	Guided missile-equipped nuclear-powered cruiser
CV	Aircraft carrier
CVGH	Guided missile-equipped helicopter carrier
CVN	Nuclear-powered aircraft carrier

DD	Destroyer
DDG	Guided missile-equipped destroyer
FF	Frigate
FFG	Guided missile-equipped frigate
LHA	Amphibious assault ship
SS	Conventionally powered attack submarine
SSB	Conventionally powered ballistic missile submarine
SSBN	Nuclear-powered ballistic missile submarine
SSGN	Nuclear-powered cruise missile submarine
SSG	Conventionally powered cruise missile submarine
SSN	Nuclear-powered attack submarine

Note on ship designations and usage

The designation of naval vessels can be most confusing to the non-specialist. An old naval system of designations has evolved into the current official US system, although it is not particularly easy for most people to use. Essentially, ships and submarines are given individual names and also 'pennant' numbers that correspond roughly to their order of construction, but they are also referred to by their 'class', which is the name or number of the first unit of a given model. To complicate matters, some vessels are also referred to by the type of equipment they carry. For example, the US ballistic missile submarine *USS Daniel Boone,* has the pennant number SSBN 629; both the name and the number are proper official designations for the submarine. But it is also a Madison Class submarine, or an SSBN 627 Class submarine, because the first submarine of that design was the *USS James Madison,* SSBN 627. And, as the submarine is armed with the Trident ballistic missile system, it can also be referred to as a 'Trident submarine'.

Soviet names present a somewhat different situation because the Soviet Navy does not reveal the names of all its vessels, particularly submarines. So a set of NATO designations is used in the West for classes of vessels for which names are not known. In the case of Soviet submarines, alphabetical class designations are used and phonetic names assigned for each class of submarine. Thus, 'Whiskey' for the W Class, 'Romeo' for the R Class, 'Charlie' for the C Class, and so on. The submarines are generally referred to by their phonetic names. As there are several classes with the same letter designation (Alfa and Akula), some names fall outside the phonetic alphabet, as is the case if the Soviet name is known—for example, the Typhoon Class ballistic missile submarine. The West uses the name of the first ship of a class if it is known, but there are many exceptions. Modifications to the design of a class are indicated by numbers, such as Victor I, Victor II and Victor III Class submarines.

Ship types are commonly designated in the West by a group of two to four letters. The letters used are from traditional naval nomenclature that is arcane but somewhat useful. They describe the type of ship (aircraft carrier=CV, battleship=BB, cruiser=C, destroyer=DD, frigate=FF, etc.) and designate certain charactertistics, such as mission, type of propulsion, type of equipment carried, and so on. For example, the letter G after ship type denotes that the vessel is equipped with a guided missile system; the letter N indicates that the vessel is powered by a nuclear reactor. For example, a CGN is a cruiser (C), equipped with guided missiles (G) and powered by a nuclear propulsion system.

Introduction and overview

Superpowers at sea: the need for a new assessment

Richard Fieldhouse

I. Introduction

The need for a new assessment

Many books have been written about naval affairs; only a few have taken naval arms control as the point of departure. This one does. It proceeds from two general observations. First, there is a naval competition between the USA and the USSR—the superpower naval arms race. Second, there are almost no arms control restraints on naval forces and activities. Consequently, the basic question is: Should and can the superpower naval arms race be brought under some measures of control or restraint, and if so, what are the possibilities and problems involved?

But before one can attempt to address or answer such a large question, it is necessary to step back and re-examine the naval arms race in order to understand some essential facts. For example, what accounts for the conspicuous lack of naval arms control? What are the fundamental characteristics of the superpower naval competition that have a bearing upon the issue of arms control at sea? In other words, what does one need to know about the two major navies in order to proceed with the basic naval arms control question? It is the purpose of this monograph to provide these facts and analyses of the superpower arms race at sea.

There are a number of reasons that suggest the need for this book now. Since the mid-1980s, there has been increased public and international interest in the naval arms race and in the possibility of naval arms control. There has been notable progress in other areas of US-Soviet arms control and co-operation on security affairs, including several new and pending arms control treaties, four summit meetings between the leaders of the USA and the USSR, and a host of other forms of co-operation on security matters. This situation highlights the fact that little is happening in naval arms control, and that there is a possibility that the arms race and nuclear weapons may move more to the seas, partly because there is so little arms control at sea. Superpower relations and arms control progress also suggest the logic of including naval forces in the general arms control, reduction and confidence-building processes. Since 1986, the Government of the USSR has emphasized its interest in naval arms control and confidence-building measures (CBMs) in a series of public speeches and articles.[1] It is even possible that some form of superpower co-operation on naval activities could be a prerequisite for success in other arms control negotiations. Finally, economic difficulties are forcing both superpowers to scale back their naval programmes somewhat. This combination of factors demonstrates that the subject of naval arms control is of growing interest and importance for the debate on peace and security. It is thus a good time to provide essential information for that debate.

II. Overview

This book concerns primarily the two superpower navies—those of the USA and the USSR. It is arranged in three parts. Part I provides a comparison of the naval forces of the USA and the USSR, and their allies. Part II offers a detailed examination and critique of the naval nuclear arms race, including the forces of the UK, France and China. And part III concludes the book with a preliminary discussion of naval arms control issues in light of the foregoing discussion of the arms race at sea. This discussion is intended to serve as a starting point for the second SIPRI book on this topic, *Security at Sea: Naval Forces and Arms Control,* which is devoted entirely to the subject of naval arms control.

Chapter 1 of the present book gives a brief historical overview of the buildup of the US and Soviet Navies. Despite considerable success in its historical ambitions to build a large and powerful navy, the USSR has never become the major naval power that such efforts might have accorded a maritime nation. By contrast, the US Navy—which has been a central element of US military power since World War II—has enjoyed relatively uninterrupted growth since the early 1970s and has a newer fleet than the USSR.

Chapter 2 (part I) provides a thorough analysis and assessment of the comparative strengths and weaknesses of the two navies, thereby dispelling the myth of Soviet naval superiority. It demonstrates that:

the US Navy has considerable advantages over the Soviet Navy, and it will maintain those advantages for the foreseeable future; the Soviet Navy is shrinking and will probably retire hundreds of ships and submarines before the year 2000; US economic pressures cast doubt on the ability of the US Navy to maintain a 600-ship fleet, but this will not reduce US advantages. It should be noted that part I was written during 1986-87, before the US Defense Department cut its own budget, including the navy's, and scaled back the plan to have 600 ships, thus proving Shunji Taoka's foresight.

Chapter 3 (part II) presents a full exposé of the naval nuclear arms race and examines its implications for armed conflict, security and arms control. It documents the widespread nuclearization of the superpower navies, the many unresolved problems, dangers and questions these weapons present, and the lack of arms control constraints on or planning for naval nuclear weapons. It focuses particularly on non-strategic naval nuclear weapons and on three related issues: the danger of nuclear war at sea, the risks of nuclear escalation, and arms control perspectives.

Chapter 4 (part III) gives an overview of the issues and possible approaches of naval arms control in relation to the future of the superpower navies. The thrust of this chapter is that both superpower navies will experience important changes and that arms control, broadly defined, may be one of the best ways to manage the change in the interests of peace and security. The chapter is meant to provide a starting point for further thought and debate on an inherently difficult and complex but important topic. It is clear that this subject has not been adequately studied, and that a great deal more thought is necessary to determine whether and how it might be possible to include naval forces in future considerations of co-operative security and arms control. All the subjects raised in chapter 4 will be treated fully in the forthcoming SIPRI volume concerning naval forces and arms control.

III.   Basic characteristics of the naval arms race

Before one can proceed with the subject of naval arms control, one must first consider the relationship between naval forces and naval arms control (or lack thereof). This requires some appreciation of the fundamental realities of the superpower naval arms race, including its nature, special characteristics, and opportunities and obstacles for naval arms control. Any attempt to achieve some form of control will require grappling with a number of serious difficulties inherent in the super-power naval competition. Three of these fundamental realities are noteworthy because they appear to be primary impediments to naval arms control.

The tremendous differences between the US and Soviet Navies, and the causes of those differences are such as to complicate greatly and diminish any prospect of agreement. The two nations have markedly different geographic, economic, political and military factors that determine their interests in or need for naval forces, as well as the kind of forces they build. For the USA these determinants result in a great reliance on the seas—some would say absolute—for economic and military security, and therefore a large and dominant navy. For the USSR the opposite is true. It depends on land routes for political, economic and military security arrangements, and has a relatively small dependence on the seas. Consequently, neither side will have the same objectives with respect to their (and their adversary's) use of the oceans and will find it difficult to agree on measures of restraint that meet the test of national interest. This means that the USA and its allies will naturally disapprove of any suggestion for restrictions or imposed restraints on their navies. This asymmetry of strategic factors and naval forces is perhaps the main challenge to naval arms control in general and to superpower naval arms control in particular.

The second reality is the nature of naval forces and the regime of the oceans they use. Navies are inherently mobile forces; they can go almost anywhere at anytime to suit the wishes of their governments. This mobility gives navies a global role that is lacking for ground or air forces, which are assigned to regions or theatres of operation or responsibility. Navies can sail where they want because of the special freedoms governing the use of the oceans. The high seas are not subject to any national jurisdiction and are basically free for all nations to use. This is the opposite of the situation on land where, with few exceptions, nations exercise absolute sovereignty and control over the use of their territory. Nations have gone to great lengths to protect the freedom of the seas. It is thus immensely difficult to place controls on the movement of military forces that are fairly free to sail in any international waters.

The third reality is simply the complexity of the subject matter. This complexity arises from the two previous factors as well as from the esoteric and obscure nature of naval forces and activities. It can be difficult for the interested observer to understand much of these affairs without some assistance. But it is also very difficult for governments or scholars to devise a scheme of controls that is feasible, equitable, useful or desirable. The sheer number and variety of naval vessels and weapons makes it hard to keep all the figures and concepts in place. Force comparisons must be made carefully in order to be useful. Moreover, navies are only one type of military force, in addition to ground and air forces. In the case of the larger naval powers, their navies include air and naval infantry elements. Naval forces must be considered as part of a nation's total military forces, whether for defence or arms control purposes. So naval arms control must be placed in the context of other arms control efforts and other military forces—a considerable task.

These three realities are enduring features of the current superpower naval arms race. But there are other basic characteristics of that arms race that are important to keep in mind when thinking about naval forces and arms control. Four of these characteristics are particularly important for this monograph. They are: the importance of naval forces; poor understanding of the naval arms race; naval nuclear weapons; and the lack of naval arms control. Each of these will be described briefly below.

Importance of superpower naval forces

Naval forces play important but remarkably different roles in the military strategies of both the USA and the USSR. For the USA, the navy is considered an essential element of national power that is used in situations from peace to war. The US Navy is oriented both towards the USSR for the contingency of a major East-West war, and towards so-called Third World hot spots or crises. For the USSR, its navy is important primarily in relation to the US and allied navies. Given the different strategic factors mentioned earlier, the USSR does not need to have superior naval forces, but sees a need to be able to defend against adversary naval forces. Because the adversary alliances depend on shipping both in peace and war, the Soviet Navy—particularly its submarines—could be used to prevent them from successfully using the seas in a war. This possibility is perhaps the only serious concern that the US and its allies have about the Soviet Navy.

One of the oldest forms of 'strategic' warfare is to block merchant shipping, either of imports or exports, to starve or isolate a nation into submission. Today maritime commerce is fundamental to the economic well-being of most industrialized and many developing nations. This fact is of increasing importance to many nations, especially given their dependence on foreign energy and resources that are shipped on the high seas. As can be seen from events in The (Persian) Gulf in recent years, shipping is one of the major concerns (and a potential target) of navies and nations alike.

In case of a war in Europe, the North Atlantic Treaty Organization (NATO) plans to ship massive quantities of men and supplies across the Atlantic from the USA to reinforce Europe (see chapter 2). Perhaps NATO's greatest fear in this event is that allied shipping would be intercepted, thus preventing a sustained conventional defence of Europe. Dominant naval forces, therefore, are considered absolutely essential to NATO. Because the USSR and its allies do not depend on sea reinforcement for defence plans, they have an entirely different set of needs for naval forces. Some in the West might go so far as to say the USSR has no need for naval forces, although this is obviously an exaggeration.

The naval competition between the USA and the USSR (and their respective allies) is part of their general military confrontation, with some noteworthy characteristics. Navies are often the first military forces on the scene of a crisis. The navies of the USA and the USSR operate in close proximity to each other on a daily basis, and are always equipped for war. The ballistic missile submarines of the USA, the USSR, France, the UK and China carry more than 9000 nuclear warheads, thus making navies a primary element of the nuclear arms race. Four of these navies are also armed with thousands of nuclear weapons for naval warfare—so-called non-strategic nuclear weapons.

Recent developments have focused new attention on the naval arms race. The USA has publicized and practiced a 'new' naval strategy that calls for the rapid destruction of the Soviet fleet and for attacks on Soviet territory, ostensibly to help prevent the USSR from winning a war in Europe (and thus dissuade its occurrence in the first place).[2] Critics decry this strategy as unduly provocative, unnecessary and unworkable, and point to the possibility that it could lead to the rapid escalation of a conflict to nuclear war.[3] The US-Soviet Intermediate-range Nuclear Forces (INF) Treaty of December 1987 banned several classes of nuclear and nuclear-capable missiles from land, but not from the sea—where both sides are currently building nuclear sea-launched cruise missiles (SLCMs). Some observers fear that the nuclear arms race may be moving increasingly from land to the sea—where there are no arms control restraints in force. All these factors point to the need to study and understand the superpower naval competition better.

Poor understanding of the naval arms race

The superpower competition at sea is not well understood. The result can be a poorly informed public and a limited debate on naval issues, which can lead to inappropriate national decisions and policies. It could also complicate or hinder efforts towards bringing naval forces or activities under some arms control or co-operative security regime.

People are often confused about or unaware of the realities of the superpowers at sea. This is easily understandable because of the considerable complexity of the topic (mentioned above) and because of partial or no information. This monograph is intended to help make the topic more easily understood.

In the West there is a large volume of partial, misleading or exaggerated information routinely publicized by otherwise well-informed bodies and governments. As Captain Richard Sharpe (RN, Ret.), editor of *Jane's Fighting Ships 1988-89,* put it: 'There is probably more nonsense talked and written at every level of classification from Top Secret to the *Washington Post* about anti-submarine warfare than any other military subject.'[4] There are a number of myths and misperceptions that permeate public debate on naval issues. These misperceptions need to be corrected if an informed public debate is to lead to rational choices and policies that improve mutual security and reduce the risk of superpower military confrontation. This monograph challenges a number of these myths.

First among the myths is the dominant strength of the Soviet Navy. In reality, as this monograph clearly demonstrates, the US Navy has significant advantages over its Soviet counterpart. The USA has a strong naval and maritime tradition and considers its naval forces to be a primary and indispensible element of its military power. For a host of reasons, the US Government believes it essential to have superior naval forces simply to carry out its minimum security obligations; anything less would be seen as unacceptable.

There are also some important aspects of naval issues that are not discussed publicly by navies or governments. Usually this takes the form of secrecy used to keep information from the public and other nations. Certain naval activities, particularly those pertaining to submarines, are among the most closely guarded superpower secrets. And almost anything relating to nuclear weapons is treated as a great secret. Ironically, although both navies are free to observe each other close-up at sea, there are many things they do not know or understand about each other. Often, the result is to assume the worst about the adversary and its forces, a process which inevitably exaggerates the true situation and deepens mutual superpower suspicion. Increasing and improving the flow of information would enhance each nation's security and the prospects for well-informed choices.

The naval nuclear arms race

The nuclear side of naval forces is not widely understood. It is not common knowledge that perhaps as many as 16 000 nuclear weapons—almost one-third of the world's total—are held by or for the navies of the five nuclear weapon states. The naval arms race is in many respects a nuclear arms race, with almost no controls in place or in mind. This is a significant omission and a potential challenge to success in current arms control efforts.

Naval nuclear weapons provide perhaps the best example of official secrecy resulting in inadequate information and understanding. Only one of the five acknowledged nuclear weapon states—the USA—makes available more than trivial information about its naval nuclear weapons. Since the USSR does not reveal any information about its naval nuclear forces, it is not even certain what weapon systems can use nuclear warheads.[5] This gap in essential public knowledge needs to be filled.

What little information is available does not permit a full debate on an important security issue. As a result, most people have no idea of the widespread nuclearization of naval forces, nor its consequences for security or arms control efforts. A few examples of the naval nuclear arms race are presented below.

There is only one type of strategic nuclear weapon system common to the five nuclear weapon states: ballistic missiles on submarines. More than 9000 nuclear warheads are carried by such missiles, and more than 6500 other warheads are estimated to be available for non-strategic naval nuclear weapons. The great majority of these naval nuclear weapons belong to the USA or to the USSR. A surprisingly large proportion of their naval vessels are capable of using nuclear weapons—about 80 per cent for the USA and more than 90 per cent for the USSR. Virtually all types of combat vessel can use nuclear weapons: ships, submarines and aircraft. Naval nuclear weapons are regularly carried by ships and submarines at sea and are stored on land for them and for land-based aircraft. These weapons are intended both for war at sea and for attacks on land targets. They have delivery ranges across the spectrum—from a few kilometres to intercontinental range—and explosive yields from sub-kiloton to multi-megaton. There are almost no arms control restraints in effect for naval nuclear weapons.

Moreover, there are many unanswered questions about official thinking and planning for non-strategic naval nuclear weapons. Although both the US and the Soviet Navies have spread nuclear weapon capabilities throughout their fleets, it is not clear why they have done so, nor why they keep weapons that seem to have little military justification. Do they believe these weapons are usable or necessary for war? Given the stakes involved, it is questionable whether political authorities would, or even could, permit the use of nuclear weapons at sea. However, there could be temptations in a war to use nuclear weapons at sea—a possibility with grave implications. The lack of either official or public study of these weapons and the many issues that they raise must be considered a serious void. Even less consideration has been given to the question of arms control for naval nuclear weapons although there are compelling reasons to pursue this subject.

No arms control at sea

Today there is very little arms control at sea and seemingly little prospect for future agreements. This is explained partly by the fact that arms control agreements cannot exist unless two or more nations see it in their interest to agree on given measures. No nation will agree to measures that it believes will diminish its security. As the USA values its navy so highly, superpower naval arms control is inherently an extremely difficult venture. Naturally, navies do not like arms control. They seem to believe that it is antithetical to their very purpose.

The lack of naval arms control is also partly explained by the unregulated nature of the oceans. No nation exercises jurisdiction over the high seas; the seas are basically free for all nations to use. Freedom of the seas is totally different from the situation on land. Many types of arms control are considered simply incompatible with the principle of freedom of the seas. Naval vessels are fairly free to go where they want and do what they want as long as they do not infringe on the freedoms and rights under international law of other states or sea traffic;

this does not mean, however, that such infringements are not made. Consequently, navies can do things that are provocative but not prohibited (e.g., suddenly to send many submarines to sea from ports; to hold sudden and unnotified exercises near an adversary's coast; to practice mock attacks against an adversary's territory; to practice tactics that disturb another nation; or to carry nuclear weapons inside the territorial waters of other nations).

Arms control at sea has a long but tarnished history. Relatively few of the measures adopted before World War II seem to have any applicability or lessons for today. Most of the current arms control that applies to the seas pertains to nuclear weapons and not to naval forces as such.[6] For example, international agreements exist that prohibit nuclear weapons from being tested underwater or from being placed on the sea-bed.[7] The Strategic Arms Limitations Talks (SALT I and II) agreements placed limits on the number of ballistic missile submarines and missile launchers for the USA and the USSR. The US-Soviet Strategic Arms Reduction Talks (START) negotiations include these strategic submarine and missile systems as well as nuclear-armed sea-launched cruise missiles. There are, however, no other arms control measures in effect or under negotiation for any other naval nuclear weapons, including those of the UK, France and China.

A few other controls exist on naval activities, but they have not normally been considered arms control—certainly not by the navies involved. The most important of these is the US-Soviet agreement of 1972 on preventing incidents at sea. The UK signed a similar agreement with the USSR in 1986, and France is reportedly negotiating one. These are basically bilateral navy-to-navy agreements that extend the normal 'rules of the road' for safe navigation and reduce the chances of poor or dangerous seamanship leading to collisions or crises. Such agreements can be considered confidence-building measures that appeal to navies because they codify and make safer the freedom of the seas. Any proposal that would restrict such freedoms will be objectionable to several maritime nations.

IV.   Conclusions

There are four major conclusions that can be drawn from this study.

First, the US Navy and its allies enjoy considerable advantages over the Soviet Navy and are likely to maintain them, perhaps even increase them, for the foreseeable future. The Soviet Navy is shrinking and will probably retire hundreds of ageing ships and submarines by the year 2000. If economic pressures continue to strain Soviet naval ship-building and operations, the Western margin of advantage will widen.

Second, non-strategic naval nuclear weapons are not necessary for the security of either the USA or the USSR. Their widespread presence throughout the superpower fleets adds dangerous problems to the task of avoiding war and could complicate current and future arms control and security efforts. Both the USA and the USSR could see com-pelling reasons for wanting to rid themselves and each other of such weapons. They should be drastically reduced and eliminated if pos-sible. This appears to be one of the most useful naval arms control goals and needs to be considered seriously.

Third, despite the large volume of naval literature, there is still room for more and better official information on these issues.[8] It could serve the interests of all concerned if the nuclear navies, most particularly the USSR, would provide more, and also more reliable, information about their forces. They should publish such information as current force structure, nuclear-capable systems, naval doctrine and strategy, and so on. Of course, much of this information is already available concerning the USA, the UK and France but not concerning their naval nuclear forces. This would improve the understanding the nations have of each other's navies, especially for the USA and the USSR, and could thus serve a confidence-building function. It would also benefit those indi-viduals who wish to take part in the debate on the relationship between naval forces, and arms control and security.

Finally, although naval arms control is an inherently difficult and complex topic and has until recently been taboo with the US Navy,[9] it could have an important role to play in the future of US-Soviet arms control and security efforts, as well as in shaping the structure of their naval forces and activities. This subject needs much more attention and analysis to determine what should and can be done. As a contribution to the debate on naval arms control and security, SIPRI has undertaken a study of the issue and will publish its results as the second volume[10] of its Project on Naval Forces and Arms Control.

Notes and references

1   These include speeches by General Secretary Gorbachev in Vladivostok (July 1986), Murmansk (October 1987) and Belgrade (March 1988). Of course, since

the early 1980s, the USSR has expressed its interest in applying confidence-building measures (CBMs) to air and naval forces at the 1980-83 Madrid follow-up meeting of the Conference on Security and Co-operation in Europe.

2   See, e.g., Watkins, J. (Adm., US Navy), 'The maritime strategy', US Naval Institute *Proceedings* (Jan. 1986), supplement, pp. 3-17.

3   Mearsheimer, J. J., 'A strategic misstep: the maritime strategy and deterrence in Europe', *International Security* (Fall 1986), vol. 11, no. 2, pp. 3-57; and Posen, B. R., 'Inadvertent nuclear war? Escalation and NATO's northern flank', *International Security* (Fall 1982), vol. 7, no. 2, pp. 28-54.

4   Sharpe, R. (ed.), *Jane's Fighting Ships—1988-89* (Jane's: London, 1988), p. 105 (from the Foreword).

5   In 1987, the Soviet Union sent a representative to Stockholm to participate in SIPRI's Conference on Naval Forces and Arms Control. But, unfortunately, despite *glasnost* in the USSR, the Soviet Government has not yet seen fit to make public specific information about its non-strategic naval nuclear weapons—among other aspects of its naval forces.

6   For a description of these measures, see *Security at Sea: Naval Forces and Arms Control*, ed. R. Fieldhouse, SIPRI (Oxford University Press: Oxford, 1989, forthcoming); and Goldblat, J., *Agreements for Arms Control: A Critical Survey*, SIPRI (Taylor & Francis: London, 1982).

7   These are: the 1963 'Treaty Banning Nuclear Weapon Tests in the Atmosphere, in Outer Space and Under Water' (also known as the Partial Test Ban Treaty, or PTBT), and the 1971 'Treaty on the Prohibition of the Emplacement of Nuclear Weapons and Other Weapons of Mass Destruction on the Seabed and the Ocean Floor and in the Subsoil Thereof' (also known as The Seabed Treaty), respectively. The texts of these treaties are contained in Goldblat (note 6), pp. 157, 175.

8   This does not concern the excellent non-official reference works available on naval forces. I am referring specifically to official government-produced information that would be exchanged and published.

9   During the course of numerous conversations with US Navy officials and a thorough search of official and public sources, it became clear to the author that until the late 1980s there was virtually nobody in the US Navy responsible for or willing to discuss publicly the issue of naval arms control. This seems to have begun changing somewhat in 1988 with the appearance of several articles by and interviews with senior US Navy officials concerning Soviet proposals, and with the establishment within the Office of the Chief of Naval Operations of an informal arms control working group.

10   Fieldhouse (note 6).

Part 1. Comparing the navies of East and West

Chapter 1. The superpower naval buildup: a brief history

Shunji Taoka

I. The naval buildup of the Soviet Union

...if a nation be so situated that it is neither forced to defend itself by land nor induced to seek extension of its territory by way of land, it has by the very unity of its aim directed upon the sea, an advantage as compared with a people one of whose boundaries is continental. This has been a great advantage to England over both France and Holland as a sea power. (*The Influence of Sea Power upon History 1660-1865*)

When Admiral A. T. Mahan (see page 24)—a historian of great influence on naval affairs—wrote this, he mainly referred to France as the typical example of a continental power, whose navy had shown a historic pattern of rise and fall. However, the rectitude of his historic observation about the co-relations between a nation's geographical location and its seapower would have been even more applicable to Russia and its navy. Though it is not the purpose of this section to discuss the history of the Russian Navy, it is necessary to take a brief look at it in order to judge accurately the implications of today's Soviet Navy and to envisage its future.

In the early part of the nineteenth century, Russia, being one of the major victors of the Napoleonic Wars, had the second largest navy, as well as the largest army, in Europe. It dominated Eastern Europe, and its attempt to expand its sphere of influence to the South, towards the Middle East, led it to collisions with Turkey and later to invade Afghanistan. Under this international political environment, which is somewhat similar to that of today, it was not surprising that a wave of 'Russo-phobia' spread in Western Europe, especially among the British and French between the 1830s and 1850s. This resulted in the dispatch of British and French fleets into the Black Sea in support of Turkey, which was under great pressure from Russia.

The Crimean War, which followed, revealed the chronic inefficiency and lack of initiative that characterized the Russian Navy during the next century. Though big in size, its Black Sea fleet was no match for the British-French fleet. Moreover, while allied troops landed on the Crimean Peninsula, the Russian fleet stayed in Sevastopol port, and before the city capitulated more than 100 warships were scuttled.[1] In the Baltic Sea, too, the British-French fleet operated as they pleased. Rather than risking its ships to counter the French landing on the island of Åland, which belonged to Finland under the Russian Empire, Russia chose to keep its principal warships in port behind strong shore defences and coastal shoals.

Despite the fact that the Russian Navy's performance in the Crimean War was a great disappointment for the Russian Tsarist Government, it put much effort and wealth into reconstructing and modernizing its navy. By 1900, the Russian Navy was second only to the British Navy in numbers of battleship.[2] It should also be noted that the newest of these battleships were mostly built in Russian shipyards, representing the considerably high level of industrialization achieved by Tsarist Russia in its final few decades.

Nevertheless, when the Russian-Japanese War ended in 1905, almost all these battleships were either sunk or captured by the Japanese, except for a few that remained in the Black Sea throughout the war.

Even this most decisive defeat did not discourage the Russian Government from rebuilding its navy. In 1913, it embarked upon a 15-year programme that included 20 battleships and 12 battle cruisers.[3] But while the programme was still in progress, Russia faced a more immediate land threat in World War I. And ensuing revolutions, civil war and foreign interventions, especially the British naval attack against the Red fleet, reduced the Russian Navy to virtual non-existence.

Without a doubt, Stalin wanted to have a large navy, one that suited the image of the great Soviet nation. Between 1927 and 1941, the Soviet Union built (or started to build) 8 battleships, 17 cruisers, 88 destroyers and 300 submarines along with many torpedo boats and mine warfare ships.[4] The Soviet Union negotiated with the United States about constructing a battleship in a US shipyard,[5] and asked the Germans to release blueprints of several types of warship, including those of the aircraft carrier *Graf Zeppelin,* which the Germans were building.[6]

With Stalin's strong push, the Soviet Navy recovered quickly from the damage of the revolutionary period, as far as the number of ships was concerned. By June 1941, when Germany attacked Russia, the

Soviet Navy had 3 battleships, 6 cruisers, 61 destroyers[7] and 218 submarines,[8] which was the largest submarine fleet in the world at the
time. Its Baltic Sea Fleet alone consisted of 2 battleships, 2 cruisers, 47
destroyers and large torpedo boats, at least 75 submarines, 110 fast
torpedo boats, and so on.[9] This was overwhelmingly larger than the
German naval force in the Baltic, which had only 5 submarines and 28
fast torpedo boats.[10] But, as usual, the Soviet Navy was not sufficiently prepared and lacked trained personnel, especially because of
Stalin's purge of senior officers between 1937 and 1938. Thus, the
Baltic fleet could not take any offensive action against the Germans
during the first months of battle, and became an easy target for German
naval and air attacks, eventually becoming bottled up in the Gulf of
Finland.

The Soviet Black Sea Fleet fought better than its counterpart in the
Baltic. It conducted several successful landings and evacuation operations, disrupted German supply lines along the Black Sea coast, and
effectively supported its army with badly needed supply transport. But
it also has to be mentioned that there was not one major German warship present in the Black Sea.

World War II claimed some 20-million Soviet lives and caused
tremendous devastation; the Soviet Union had to expend almost all of
its resources to rebuild its ground and air forces in order to push back
the mighty German forces. The Soviet fleet again found itself in a
shambles and most of its shipyards in ruins. But almost immediately
after the war, Stalin resumed his pre-war ambition to build a large navy.
The necessity of a navy in the approaching Soviet confrontation with
the United States, which soon followed their victory against the Axis
powers, endorsed his naval dream. Lacking a navy, the Soviet Union
was certainly in a very vulnerable position to attacks by US aircraft
carriers and amphibious forces. Stalin again drove the war-weary
Soviet people and the still recovering economy to the reconstruction of
its navy.

Stalin's plan was so grandiose that it looks almost megalomaniac by
present standards. Reportedly, it included 1200 submarines,[11] 4 battle
cruisers (40 000 t class), 16 heavy cruisers and 24 cruisers.[12] His
plan looks anachronistic as well, because ship design of the period
reflected pre-World War II concepts of sea combat, although this might
have been inevitable judging from the standard of Soviet naval technologies of the day and the lack of naval warfare experience from the
war. In the post-war Stalin era, 24 of the Sverdlov Class cruisers

(16 000 t, 152 mm Gun x 12) were ordered and 17 of them were completed, together with nearly 240 Whiskey Class submarines before Khrushchev stopped the programme. In 1955 and 1956 alone more than 120 Whiskey Class submarines, plus 37 submarines of other types, were built. The successor to the Whiskey Class—the Romeo Class—was intended to be mass produced in even more staggering numbers—560 boats[13]—although this project too was suspended in the Khrushchev period and only 20 Romeo Class submarines were actually commissioned.

The US Navy, in the meantime, had built its first nuclear-powered submarine, the *USS Nautilus,* in 1954 and thus pushed all diesel-electric-powered submarines, which the Soviet Union was building in large numbers, into obsolescence.

In 1956, Khrushchev, who openly criticized large surface ships and referred to them as 'coffins',[14] chose a young admiral, named Admiral S. G. Gorshkov, who had distinguished himself in the Black Sea during the war, as his Commander-in-Chief of the Soviet Navy. Gorshkov was given the task of modernizing the Soviet Navy. Under his energetic guidance, which lasted until 1985, the Soviet Navy was transformed from an anachronistic navy to a modern, missile-carrying, nuclear-armed and -powered, and aircraft-capable navy. (In view of the fact that the Soviet Navy's large-scale reconstruction programme was started in the 1950s, one must question the widespread view that the Cuban Missile Crisis in 1962—in which the US Navy blockaded the island and forced Soviet cargo ships carrying SS-4s to return home—humiliated the Soviet Union and triggered its naval buildup).

When Admiral Gorshkov was appointed Commander-in-Chief of the Soviet Navy, it mostly consisted of World War II type submarines and pre-World War II type surface ships. For example, the design of Sverdlov Class cruisers strongly reflected the influence of the Italian Zara Class cruisers completed between 1931 and 1932. Of course the Soviet Union had no nuclear-powered submarines and no missile-carrying ships. And lacking an aircraft-capable ship, the Soviet Navy could be regarded as a coastal defence navy, whose diesel-electric-powered submarines and land-based aviation could become a threat to the US fleet only if it came too close to Soviet shores.

In the 30 years since, the Soviet Navy has shown a remarkable growth both in quantity and quality, although it has to be mentioned that the Soviet Navy's modernization had probably started while Gorshkov was still the Commander of the Black Sea Fleet before being promoted to Commander-in-Chief in 1956. The first Soviet nuclear-powered submarine, the November Class, was completed in 1958, and in 1960 the Soviet Navy had the world's first anti-ship missile-carrying destroyer, the Kildin Class. In any country it would take years to develop a radically new weapon system, such as nuclear propulsion or an anti-ship missile. The navy has to have the ship construction programme approved by the government and get necessary funding. Then it needs at least another few years for shipyards to build a prototype ship. Therefore, it would not be correct to give Admiral Gorshkov all of the credit for the Soviet Navy's expansion and modernization. Rather, it should be regarded as having been a continuous effort since Stalin's era.

Nevertheless, it cannot be denied that Admiral Gorshkov was a proponent of a big navy and fought fiercely with the army-dominated Soviet military hierarchy, writing numerous books and articles to rally support for his navy. He was doubtlessly the tireless arch-public relations officer of the Soviet Navy and succeeded in maintaining its course of expansion and modernization for three decades, in spite of many hurdles, such as the economic constraints of the Soviet nation, technological gaps and natural skepticism towards the navy's value for Soviet defence. Admiral Gorshkov will perhaps remain in naval history abreast with Admiral Tirpitz, the founder of the German High-Sea Fleet before World War I; however, in both cases, it can be argued whether or not their naval buildups could and would contribute to their national security as a whole.

In his article in *Krasnaiia Zvezda (Red Star)* of 7 July 1984, Admiral Gorshkov spoke about the 'dramatic increase' of the Soviet Navy since the 1960s from a coastal navy to an ocean-going navy and said:

...the oceans which once protected America from retaliatory strikes from the victims of aggression have completely lost their value as defensive barriers... Concentrated in current ships are all the essential factors to determine the combat strength of today's navy; large strike power, high mobility, the capability to conduct battle operations on a global scale in various regions of the world oceans against the hostile navy and the implementation of destructive missions against important land targets.

What he said is not untrue. And it is understandable that he was proud of what he had achieved in 29 years. In 1956, the Soviet Navy's largest ships were Kirov Class cruisers of pre-war construction and Sverdlov Class of pre-war concept. Now they have four aircraft carriers of the Kiev Class (37 100 t, full load) and are building bigger ones (65 000 t) even though their capabilities will not be as good as the USA's existing ones, let alone the newest carriers (see chapter 2).

In the area of sea-launched anti-ship missiles, the Soviet Navy has led the navies of the world.[15] After the Kildin Class missile-equipped destroyers, a series of missile-carrying cruisers such as the Kynda Class, the Kresta I and II Classes, and the Kara Class were built, culminating in the Kirov Class nuclear-powered missile cruiser, with a displacement 22 000 t, and the Slava Class missile cruiser. In October 1967, Egypt used a Soviet-built Komar Class patrol boat and a Styx anti-ship missile to sink the Israeli destroyer *Eilat*. This incident proved the Soviet Navy's rationale for developing anti-ship missiles. It also triggered world-wide changes in naval ordnance and tactics. The adoption of anti-ship missiles by the Soviet Navy was a revolutionary event in naval history that can perhaps be compared to the introduction of explosive shells to naval artillery, which was also done by the Russian Navy in the nineteenth century.

In the submarine field, the progress of the Soviet Navy in this 30-year period is more obvious. In 1956, Admiral Gorshkov had 240 Whiskey Class submarines and 28 of the Zulu Class, along with many obsolete submarines including Sierra-type boats, designed before World War II. In 1958, the Soviet Navy had its first nuclear-powered submarine of the November type. It is now believed to have 187 nuclear-powered submarines of various types, almost 40 per cent more than the US submarine fleet which has 135 nuclear-powered submarines, although it is qualitatively still inferior to US submarines in many respects (see chapter 2).

Putting aside these quality questions for the moment, the quantitative growth of the Soviet Navy has been amazing. In the 10 years between 1976 and 1986, its total tonnage of submarines, aircraft carriers and major surface combatants (cruisers, destroyers, frigates bigger than 1000 tons in full-load condition, excluding KGB patrol ships) has increased from 2 474 000 t to 3 428 000 t, showing a 38.6 per cent increase, while that of the US Navy (excluding Coast Guard 'cutters'), increased from 2 628 000 t to 3 488 000 t, showing 32.7 per cent growth for the same period.

The Soviet Navy was also ahead of the US Navy in the number of submarine-launched ballistic missiles (SLBMs). Between 1955 and 1957 it converted six Zulu Class submarines to carry two 500-km range ballistic missiles. But in 1959, the *USS George Washington,* the first

'Polaris' submarine-launched ballistic missile (SLBM)-carrying nuclear-powered submarine was commissioned, giving a long lead to the United States. And in 1962 the Soviet Union commissioned the Hotel Class, its first nuclear-powered ballistic missile submarine. In 1967 the Yankee Class nuclear-powered submarine with 16 missiles was first deployed, which was roughly equal to the US Polaris submarines.

The deployment of the Delta Class in 1972, with 12 SS-N-8 missiles having an intercontinental range of 7800 km, first gave the Soviet Union a truly survivable strategic second-strike capability, being able to strike targets in the continental United States from Soviet coastal waters almost immune to US anti-submarine operations. The Typhoon Class submarines, which the Soviet Union is now building in series, along with the newest version of the Delta IV Class, have a submerged displacement of 25 000 t and are equipped with 20 SS-N-20 missiles (range: 8300 km), carrying 10 warheads each. This is the largest submarine ever built, although compared with US Ohio Class submarines (18 700 t submerged, 24 Trident missiles), the enormous size of the Typhoon Class is not an indication of its superiority. Bigger sizes of Soviet naval weapon systems, in general, relative to comparable Western naval weapons, can at least be partly attributed to the technological weakness of Soviet industry, especially in the area of microelectronics.

But such rapid quantitative growth of the Soviet Navy is now becoming a thing of the past, as a large number of ships (about 180 submarines and 140 major surface combatants which were mass produced in the 1950s and 1960s) are expected to be retired before 1997, reaching the end of a warship's normal service life of 30 years. By the end of this century, 60 other Soviet submarines and 50 surface combatants will follow suit.

The pace of Soviet shipbuilding has apparently slowed down in recent years to an average rate of six to eight submarines and six major surface combat ships a year. If this pace continues, it appears impossible for the Soviet Navy to make up for the impending block retirement of obsolete ships. Though each new ship and submarine is of course larger and more capable than older ones, the Soviet Navy will shrink while the US Navy and some of its allied navies are gradually increasing both in numbers and quality.

This situation is similar to the problem that the US Navy faced in the early 1970s, when most of the ships it built in World War II, especially destroyers, had to be decommissioned almost simultaneously. The period coincided with the long, unsuccessful and costly foreign military intervention in Viet Nam which resulted in a minimum of new ship orders in the late 1960s.

In spite of the fact that Soviet war costs in Afghanistan are presumably much less than were those of the United States in Viet Nam, the burden of the Afghanistan war costs on the economy and the seemingly overstretched military budget cannot be ignored.

Then the navy, the smallest brother in the Soviet military family, and in particular its surface force, might become the first to suffer from resource constraints.

II. The naval buildup of the United States

There is no doubt that the US Navy has been a good student of the dictum of Alfred T. Mahan (see page 17), who contended that the United States should build a strong navy for its commercial and industrial success. His books found many ardent readers among national leaders in the early twentieth century, including Germans and Japanese, the result of which often led to naval confrontations between 'Mahanist' nations. Mahan himself, however, was perhaps not so much a direct supporter of colonial expansion.

In his book—*The Influence of Sea Power upon History 1660-1865*—published in 1890, Mahan expressed the hope that a strong US Navy 'will not come to birth too late' and that the USA would have naval bases in the Caribbean Sea. As he hoped, the US Navy expanded very rapidly in the last decade of the nineteenth century. This new naval might enabled the United States to invade Cuba in 1898 and to seize the Philippines and other Spanish overseas possessions. In the same year the USA annexed Hawaii, thus becoming one of the colonial powers.

The end of World War II saw the materialization of Mahanist ideals. US naval strength was by far superior to the combined strength of all other navies of the world. In 1945, it had 37 regular aircraft carriers, 77 escort aircraft carriers converted from merchant ships, 24 battleships, 911 destroyers/escort destroyers and 267 submarines. In addition, the United States had the only atomic bombs, an overwhelming air force, and, above all, enormous economic strength to support this military power. All of this was achieved within the 30 years following the death of Mahan.

However, this unquestioned dominance of the seas by the US Navy, which lasted for more than 20 years from 1945, was first over-shadowed by the Viet Nam War. The direct loss of US warships in the war was almost zero (on 17 July 1972, the destroyer *USS Warrington* was damaged beyond repair when it hit a mine that had been laid by a US aircraft perhaps days before). But financially the war did tremendous damage to the US Navy. In fiscal year (FY) 1969, when the US involvement in Viet Nam was at its peak, the US Navy's ship construction budget dropped to $1-billion, which, in constant value, was one-fifth of the sum in 1962, the year before the United States fully committed itself to the war in Viet Nam. This was mostly due to the increase of the US Army and Air Force budget share of the overall defence budget and to the direct war costs of the navy itself, such as fuel, ordnance and human costs associated with overseas combat duty.

The 1970s was also the time when the ships built during World War II were coming to the end of their service lives of about 30 years. The Soviet Navy, however, had few problems with obsolecence because it started its naval buildup in the 1950s, about 10 years after the US Navy's massive shipbuilding programme. Thus, Soviet warships were rapidly growing in number, while the number of US ships was decreasing.

As newer and bigger ships came into the Soviet Navy, its operations were becoming more blue-water-oriented (a term for broad oceans) to the point where the navy could conduct global naval exercises such as Okean 70 (in 1970) and Okean 75 (in 1975). It is understandable that US Navy leaders in this period were irritated to see their fleet shrinking while the Soviet fleet continued to expand, thus they began to emphasize the 'navy gap' between the USA and the USSR. Shortly before his retirement, in 1974, Admiral E. R. Zumwalt, the US Chief of Naval Operations (CNO), stated during the TV programme 'Meet the Press' that the US Navy had lost its sea control ability, and if forced to fight the Soviet Navy with conventional weapons, it might lose. He went so far as to say that it would be wiser for US fleet commanders to keep their fleets from possible conflict areas. But while these views were often expressed in public, in reality the US Navy was rapidly recovering from the invisible economic damages of the Viet Nam War period as the United States withdrew more of its troops from Viet Nam. In 1970, the shipbuilding budget was increased to $2.5-billion from $1-billion the previous year, and in 1973, the year of complete withdrawal, it reached $3-billion.

Since then, the US Navy has continued an almost uninterrupted growth, as symbolized by the large-scale construction of 31 Spruance Class destroyers in 8 years, and 51 Oliver Hazard Perry Class frigates in 11 years. Although the Carter Administration tried to reduce defence spending and to cut the shipbuilding programme of the Ford Administration from 157 to 70 ships over a five-year period, even this lower (and controversial) figure resulted in a considerable increase and rapid modernization of the US fleet. The shipbuilding programme started under the Ford Administration had aimed at building 157 ships in the five-year period between 1978 to 1982, including 2 nuclear-powered aircraft carriers, 8 Trident missile-carrying strategic nuclear-powered submarines, 8 nuclear-powered attack (anti-submarine/anti-ship) submarines, 8 nuclear-powered cruisers, 10 guided-missile destroyers and 58 frigates. But the Carter Administration in 1978 cut the shipbuilding programme down to 70 ships, including 1 nuclear-powered aircraft carrier, 6 Trident missile-carrying strategic nuclear-powered submarines, 5 nuclear-powered attack submarines, 7 guided-missile destroyers and 26 frigates, among others. While the programme under the Ford Administration aimed at a 600-ship navy, the Carter Administration's plan, which envisaged only 500 ships, caused an inevitable uproar among navy leaders.

US Secretary of Defense Casper Weinberger stated in his Annual Report to Congress for FY 1985: 'Starting with 479 deployable battle force ships in late 1980, the Navy's fleet is projected to grow to 545 ships by the end of FY 1985.'[16] This statement could give the public the impression of a rapid growth in the US Fleet as a result of the policies of the first four years of the Reagan Administration. As a matter of fact, most of the ships that came into service in this period were the ones ordered before the Reagan Administration began in 1981, with the exception of two of the four Iowa Class battleships, whose reactivation the Reagan Administration ordered. The construction time of a US aircraft carrier is about seven years after the keel is laid, and about three years for a cruiser or destroyer. Moreover, after the initial funding, two years lead time is needed before the construction starts. Therefore it is wrong to attribute the US Navy's expansion in the early half of the 1980s to the policy of the Reagan Administration. Nevertheless, there can be no doubt that the Reagan Administration has promoted a policy of naval force expansion.

Basically, the Reagan Administration only reaccelerated the trend of US Navy expansion. Again aiming for a 600-ship navy, it chose drastic measures, such as ordering two nuclear-powered aircraft carriers simultaneously, with a cost of $6559.5-million, in FY 1983, and again in FY 1987 it approved the lead orders for two more carriers. The US shipbuilding plan from FY 1987 to FY 1991 includes 5 Trident Class submarines, 15 nuclear-powered attack submarines, 8 guided-missile cruisers and 17 guided-missile destroyers. By the mid-1990s, the US Navy's fleet of active ships is expected to reach 600 ships. This exceeds the figure of 585 ships proposed by the most ambitious 'option III' in the 'Seaplan 2000' prepared in 1978. Option III of the study was aimed at superiority over the future Soviet Navy.

But there is a question about whether this force level of 600 ships can be maintained in light of the large costs entailed and the economic restrictions on the unprecedented rate of growth for defence spending. This has and will continue to affect the US Navy. The navy estimates that it would take a 3 per cent real growth navy budget to sustain/maintain the 600-ship navy. The navy budgets for FY 1986 and FY 1987 were not fully funded by the US Congress even at those relatively low growth rates. There is little prospect that the budget situation will improve in the foreseeable future.

At the higher level of the US national economy, there are also warning signs. The US Government deficit reached $2.1-million in 1987, and the US overseas debt climbed to $200-billion. The International Monetary Fund (IMF) has estimated that this latter figure will reach $1-trillion by the early 1990s. Given a financial and economic situation of these proportions, one must ask whether the United States will be able to maintain a 600-ship navy.

Notes and references

1   Pemsel, H., *Atlas of Naval Warfare* (Arms and Armour Press: London, 1977), p. 90.
2   Tsouras, P., 'Soviet naval tradition', *The Soviet Navy, Strength and Liabilities*, ed. B. Watson and S. Watson (Westview Press: Boulder, CO, 1986), p. 11.
3   Mitchel, D. W., *A History of Russian and Soviet Sea Power* (André Deutsch Ltd: London, 1974), p. 274.
4   *Conway's All the World's Fighting Ships 1922-1946* (Conway Maritime Press: London, 1980), p. 320.
5   Mitchel (note 3), p. 366.
6   Moore, J., *The Soviet Navy Today* (Macdonald and Jane's Publishing Co.: London, 1975), p. 63.

7 Pemsel (note 1), p. 115.

8 Tsouras (note 2), p. 57.

9 Mitchel (note 3), p. 385.

10 Mitchel (note 3), p. 385.

11 *Conway's All the World's Fighting Ships 1947-82, Part II* (Conway Maritime Press: London, 1983), p. 467.

12 *Conway's* (note 11), p. 481.

13 *Jane's Fighting Ships 1986-87* (Jane's Publishing Co.: London, 1986), p. 554.

14 *Conway's* (note 11), p. 465.

15 It should be mentioned, however, that during World War II the German Air Force used radio-controlled and rocket-propelled air-to-surface missiles.

16 *Report of the Secretary of Defense Caspar W. Weinberger to the Congress on the FY 1985 budget, FY 1986 Authorization Request and FY 1985-89 Defense Programs, February 1, 1984,* Hearings before a Subcommittee of the Committee on Appropriations, House of Representatives, 98th Congress, Second Session (US Government Printing Office: Washington, DC, 1984), Part 1, p. 123.

Chapter 2. East-West naval force comparison

Shunji Taoka

I. Introduction

One of the focal questions in the discussion of the naval arms race should be the relative strength of the navies of the two military super-powers and their allies. The accurate assessment and comparison of their real capabilities and problems, at present and in the foreseeable future, is essential for any study concerning the possibilities of naval arms control. At the same time, whether or not the Soviet Navy is, or is going to be, stronger than the US Navy and its allied navies, as asserted and feared by some, is a factor of major significance for many defence thinkers who try to pursue rational security policies for each of their countries.

However, numerical force comparisons, which have become a central practice in defence and arms control analysis, and particularly so with strategic nuclear forces, are irrelevant because of a number of reasons including:

1. The navies of the United States and its allies, and that of the Soviet Union, are asymmetrical in character, reflecting different geopolitical and economic backgrounds, while the strategic nuclear forces of each country are basically similar, in concepts and functions.

2. The roles and missions that navies are expected to perform are quite diversified, whereas strategic nuclear forces have one main deterrent role.

3. Aside from numbers of warships and naval aircraft or total ship tonnage, there are numerous critically important factors in assessing the capability of a navy, including, *inter alia,* the qualities of naval airpower and equipment, training of personnel, operational rates, naval bases, repair facilities and geographical conditions.

These reasons make static force comparisons, which can be fairly relevant in discussing strategic nuclear arms, less valid when thinking about the naval power balance. Though numerical force comparisons are indispensable, the need for the comparison and assessment of other factors is also obvious.

One of the ways to make valid comparisons is to analyse relative capabilities of navies according to the functions they are required to perform, such as sea surface control, anti-air warfare, submarine warfare and anti-submarine warfare. Of course, the sea-based nuclear role is extremely important for navies (see part II, chapter 3). The following sections offer such an analysis.

II. Sea surface control

Nowadays, it is more popular to use the term 'sea control' instead of the more traditional expression 'command of the sea'. The logic behind this is that a superior navy cannot expect an undisputed 'command' of the sea in modern sea warfare because of the emergence of submarines and aircraft in naval warfare. But naval history tells us that even in the days of sailing ships, superior navies have rarely gained an absolute command of the sea. For example, during the war of American independence, American privateers captured nearly 3000 British merchant ships in spite of the general dominance of the British Fleet in the Atlantic. Until the nineteenth century, privateers, who were like pirates with government licence, played a role similar to that of submarines in World Wars I and II. Even as late as the early part of World War II, until long-range maritime patrol planes equipped with radars were extensively deployed, German surface raiders, such as the pocket battleship *Grafspee*, could cruise the Atlantic and Indian Oceans and threaten allied sea commerce. Because a mast-top look-out could find a ship within only a 30-km radius under optimum conditions, a fast warship could play a hide-and-seek game with a superior enemy fleet. So actually the introduction of aircraft to navies has helped superior navies to gain even greater command on the surface of the high seas, rather than complicating the problem.

Thus, since World War II, the command of the sea, or surface sea control, has become almost a synonym for the command of the air, or in modern terms 'air superiority' above sea surface. The sinking of the German battleship, the *Bismark*, in May 1941, in which obsolete British 'Swordfish' torpedo bombers played an important part by damaging her starboard rudder, and the sinking of the two British battleships, the *Prince of Wales* and the *Repulse*, off Malaya in

December 1941, by the Japanese Navy's land-based bombers, became unquestionable proof that surface ships lacking air cover were obviously easy targets for attacking aircraft.

Because only aircraft carriers are capable of providing air cover above the sea, outside of coastal waters and outside the reach of land-based fighters, aircraft-carrier strength (that is, the number of aircraft carriers, and the number of aircraft aboard, their quality, pilot training, and so on) has been the decisive factor in sea control since World War II.

Aircraft carriers

In this very important category of naval force, the US Navy has overwhelming superiority over the Soviet Navy. The US Navy has 5 nuclear-powered aircraft carriers and 10 conventionally powered ones (plus 3 obsolete carriers which are retained for training and reserve purposes). By 1992, the US Navy will have 7 nuclear-powered aircraft carriers and 8 conventionally powered ones, excluding carriers for training and reserve. The newest of the US aircraft carriers are the Nimitz Class ships which have about 91 000 t displacement (full load). The construction cost of each of the two ships ordered in 1983 is $3258-million. (This, of course, does not include the costs of the aircraft to be carried aboard, which will again be about half the ships' construction costs.)

Of all the 14 active carriers, 7 are currently assigned to the Atlantic/Mediterranean and 7 are in the Pacific/Indian Oceans. One of the conventionally powered aircraft carriers is, by rotation, receiving a modernization refit for 28 months, in order to extend its service life to 45 years from the 30 years originally planned.

The US Atlantic Fleet (headquarters {HQ}: Norfork, VA) has the 2nd Fleet under its command, usually with 5 aircraft carriers, while the US Naval Forces in Europe (HQ: London) commands the 6th Fleet in the Mediterranean Sea usually with 2 aircraft carriers and about 14 escorts, although the number of aircraft-carrier battle groups assigned to each Fleet (2nd and 6th) is not fixed and varies according to situations.

The US Pacific Fleet (HQ: Pearl Harbor, Hawaii) has two fleets. Its 7th Fleet is responsible for the Western Pacific (west of 160°E) and Indian (east of 17°E) Oceans with two aircraft-carrier battle groups, while the 3rd Fleet covers the Eastern Pacific Ocean and the Bering Sea, and at the same time functions as a training unit with four carrier groups. In a critical situation, the US 6th and 7th Fleets, in the front line of possible conflict, can be reinforced in two or three weeks by 2nd and 3rd Fleet ships dispatched from home waters.

It would be possible for the US Navy to deploy up to five aircraft carrier battle groups both in the Western Pacific and European waters in about three weeks. (In the 'Fleetex 85' exercise in November 1984, the US Navy concentrated five aircraft carriers in the Western Pacific for a simulated attack of the Soviet Pacific coast).

Typical air wings aboard a US aircraft carrier have 86 or more aircraft. They are composed of 24 F-14As (fighter aircraft), 24 A-7Es (attack aircraft), 10 A-6Es (all-weather attack aircraft), 4 KA-6Ds (tanker aircraft for in-flight refuelling), 4 E-2Cs (airborne early warning aircraft with large air-search radar), 10 S-3As (anti-submarine aircraft), 4 EA-6Bs (electronic warfare aircraft to jam an opponent's radar, radio communication, missile guidance, etc.), 6 SH-3Ds (anti-submarine helicopters), and sometimes 1 or 2 EA-3Bs (electronic intelligence aircraft) are included (see table 1). This means that one aircraft carrier has 58 fighter/attack aircraft in total, and 10 S-3As, which are capable of carrying two 'Harpoon' anti-ship missiles and can be used for anti-ship attacks, if necessary. In the future, A-7Es will be replaced by F/A-18As (fighter/attack aircraft) and carrier air wings will have major reorganizations. The new carrier air wing organization will consist of 20 F-14s, 20 F/A-18s, 20 A-6E/Fs, 5 EA-6Bs, 5 E-2Cs, 10 S-3A/Bs, and 6 SH-3Hs or 6 new SH-60F ASW helicopters.

The Soviet Navy, however, has four Kiev Class aircraft carriers (37 100 t, full load). Two of them are in its Pacific Fleet (HQ: Vladivostok), one is in the Northern Fleet (HQ: Severomorsk) and the fourth one, whose construction was possibly finished in 1986, is in the Black Sea and has not come out to the Mediterranean as of year-end 1987.

Although Kiev Class ships are classified as 'aircraft carriers' by Western navies, they are different from US aircraft carriers in that they lack catapults and arresting wires indispensable to launch and recover high performance conventional take-off and landing (CTOL) jet aircraft. Instead, they carry 13 Yak-38 (Forger) vertical take-off and landing (VTOL) planes, and 19 Ka-25 (Hormone) or Ka-32 (Helix) helicopters, mainly intended for anti-submarine purposes.

Table 1. **Comparison of US and Soviet carrier air wings**

US (Nimitz Class):

Number	Type
24	F-14A (fighter)
24	A-7E (attack)
10	A-6E (all-weather attack)
4	E-2C (early warning)
4	EA-6B (electronic warfare)
4	KA-6 (refuelling)
10	S-3A (anti-submarine warfare)
6	SH-3H (anti-submarine helicopter)
86	

*Fixed-wing aircraft total 80
*For anti-air/anti-surface warfare one US CV can use 68 aircraft
  (S-3As can carry 'Harpoon' ASMs)
*1 or 2 EA-3B (Elint) often embarked aboard CVs in 6th and 7th fleets
*14 US CVs carry about 1100 fixed-wing aircraft, 800 of which are
  fighter/attack

USSR (Kiev Class):

Number	Type
13	Yak-38 'Forger' (V/STOL) aircraft
16	Ka-25 'Hormone' A
	or Ka-27 'Helix' A (ASW helicopter)
3	Ka-25 'Hormone' B (target acquisition)
32	

*Fixed-wing aircraft total 13
*4 Soviet CVs carry 52 fixed-wing aircraft

Although VTOL and V/STOL (for vertical/short take-off and landing) planes have the inherent advantage of being able to operate from a ship's deck without special launching/recovery equipment, or from a short landing pad on ground, compared to CTOL aircraft they have inevitable limitations in performance, such as range, payload and maximum speed. At present there are four types of V/STOL fixed-wing aircraft used in the world: the Harrier (UK); Sea Harrier (UK); AV-8B (USA; advanced version of Harrier); and the Forger (USSR). But the Forger is very different from the Harrier family of aircraft in that it has two lift jet engines that have been installed in a nearly vertical position just aft the cockpit. These lift jets are used only for take-off and landing, whereas the Harriers use one jet engine with 'vectored thrust', which has four swivel nozzles on the side of the fuselage. This difference means that: *(a)* the Forger's two lift jets occupy the precious space behind the cockpit, which would otherwise be used for fuel tanks; *(b)* the Forger's lift jet will become dead weight after take-off; and *(c)* Harriers can make rolling take-offs, having jet nozzles in oblique positions and are usually operated as short take-off and vertical-landing aircraft. By doing this they can drastically increase their take-off weight compared with vertical take-off, and be able to carry more weapons or fuel. Forgers, however, are generally operated, at least in earlier versions, in vertical take-off mode, because they rely on lift jets.

Consequently, Forgers have to be much inferior in range and payload to Harriers, to say nothing of the CTOL combat aircraft of the US Navy. In an attack mission, the Forger's combat radius is generally estimated to be less than 320 km by Western sources,[1] but there was even a report which said that the Forger's maximum observed flight time was only 16 minutes.[2] The Western estimation is that its maximum weapon load is 1350 kg and its maximum speed is Mach 1.1.[3] It lacks a search radar, which is necessary for anti-ship attacks or air-to-air combat in all-weather conditions. For air-to-air combat, it can carry only two short-range infra-red homing missiles and a gun pod (see table 2).

The US Navy's carrier-borne aircraft are superior to Forgers in almost any category of performance. The F-14A fighter, for example, has a maximum speed in excess of Mach 2; its practical combat radius is over 800 km, and it has long-range radar and advanced fire control systems that can simultaneously guide six long-range (130 km) Phoenix air-to-air missiles to six different targets. A-6E attack aircraft can attack any target within a radius of at least 800 kms from the carrier, flying at

Table 2.   Characteristics of US and Soviet carrier-borne combat aircraft

---

F-14A Tomcat (US Navy):
Speed:	Mach 2.4 (at 11 000 m); Mach 1.2 (at surface level)
Combat radius:	740-830 km
Missiles:	6 x AIM 54 (range: 130 km)
	2 x AIM 9 (range: 18 km)
Radar:	AWG 9 (range: more than 180 km)
Gun:	20-mm Vulcan (676 rounds)

A-6E Intruder (US Navy):
Speed:	Mach 0.86 (at surface level)
Combat radius:	740 km+ (maximum payload)
Armament:	30 x 225-kg bombs (maximum capacity 8165 kg)
Radar:	APQ-156 multi-mode (for all-weather, day/night attack

AV-8B Harrier II (US Marine Corps):
Speed:	668 knots (at surface level)
Combat radius:	1100 km (with 7 x 225-kg bombs)
Armament:	(Maximum) 16 x 225-kg bombs
Missile:	4 x AIM 9 (range: 18 km)
Gun:	25-mm multibarrel (300 rounds)

Yak-38 Forger (Soviet Navy):
Speed:	Mach ~1.1 (at 10 000 m);
	Mach 0.85 (at surface level) = 560 knots
Combat radius:	270 km (~16 minutes)
Missiles:	2 x AA8 (range: ~8 km)
Radar:	Small ranging radar
Gun:	Twin 23 mm (gun pod)

---

very low altitudes to avoid radar detection. It can carry more than 8000 kg of weapons.

While 14 US aircraft carriers (excluding one in dockyard for refitting under the Service Life Extension Programme) carry about 1100 of these high-performance fixed-wing aircraft that are operated by extremely well-trained and experienced crews; 4 Soviet aircraft carriers, in total, can carry only 52 fixed-wing aircraft whose real value in combat is at best questionable. This makes the attempt to compare the US air-craft-carrier force with that of the Soviet Union almost ridiculous.

Soviet aircraft carriers can even be regarded as inferior to the two ageing French Clemenceau Class aircraft carriers that carry about 10 supersonic Crusader fighters and 20 Super Etendard attack aircraft. The Kiev Class can be outranged by US Tarawa Class amphibious assault ships (39 300 t, full load) that can operate AV8A/B Harriers (which are obviously superior to Forgers).

The three British Invincible Class light aircraft carriers (CVL) (19 500 t, full load); the new Spanish CVL, the *Principe De Auturias* (15 150 t, full load); and the new Italian CVL, the *Giuseppe Garibaldi* (13 320 t, full load) can operate Sea Harrier aircraft. Also, the US Navy's three training/reserve carriers, formerly of the Essex Class (40 000 t), which can operate supersonic fighters, are doubtlessly superior to the Kiev Class. Even Argentina's obsolete *Veinticinco De Mayo* (19 866 t, full load) may be better than a Soviet aircraft carrier, because she carries French-built Super Etendard attack aircraft, which have a much longer range, a search radar and Exocet anti-ship missiles.

Since there is such a tremendous disparity in aircraft-carrier strength between the United States (and its allies) and the Soviet Union, a series of new and impressive-looking Soviet surface ships, such as the Kirov Class 'cruisers', (28 000 t, full load) or the Slava Class cruisers (12 500 t, full load), would be extremely vulnerable in wartime situations. It would be suicidal for these ships to come out beyond the combat radius of Soviet land-based aircraft in wartime to confront the US Fleet. These Soviet surface ships, as well as their aircraft carriers, would have to keep in their harbours or in coastal waters if they were to avoid quick destruction in a conventional war.

To make up for the lack of sea-based air power, the Kiev Class carriers, as well as many Soviet cruisers and destroyers, are equipped with anti-ship missiles. The Kiev Class ships have eight launchers for SS-N-12 anti-ship missiles with an estimated range of 550 km. But since the ships' radars cannot detect anything beyond the horizon (which is less than 60 km from the Kiev's mast-top antennae to another ship's mast), the Soviet Navy apparently needs a spotting aircraft (or submarine) that locates targets and gives their positions, course and speed to missile-launching ships. For this target acquisition role, a Kiev Class ship carries a few 'Hormone B' helicopters equipped with search radars.

But in order for a Soviet helicopter to locate a US aircraft carrier, it would have to approach as close as 250 km to the target, assuming that it is flying at an altitude of 3000 m. Although aircraft often fly very close to a foreign navy's ships in peacetime and take photographs of each other, it is very unlikely that the US Navy would let a Soviet helicopter fly around its fleets after hostilities have started or a situation has become tense. Thus, the only situation in which Soviet long-range ship-to-ship missiles might be effective would be in a surprise attack scenario. (Therefore, there is a danger that US Navy reactions to prevent such a surprise attack, the so-called 'battle of the first salvo', could provoke an escalation. For example, US Fleet commanders might, under tense situations, try to chase away Soviet aircraft, perhaps even firing warning shots.) If a collision or excessive harassment of each other happens at a time when international tensions have mounted, it might lead to an accidental armed conflict between the two military superpowers.

There is an apparent need for some measures to prevent such incidents. The Incidents at Sea Agreement signed in 1972 between the United States and the Soviet Union and in 1986 between the United Kingdom and the Soviet Union are mainly aimed at preventing collisions of ships, but have some value in confidence-building. However, these agreements cannot guarantee the prevention of accidental war at sea.

In addition to its four VTOL carriers, the Soviet Navy has been building one or two large (possibly nuclear-powered) aircraft carriers in the Nikolayev South shipyard on the Black Sea since 1983. Because of its size, which is estimated to be about 65 000 t, it was naturally assumed to be a regular aircraft carrier equipped with catapults and arresting gears, which are necessary to operate high-performance CTOL aircraft. However, it is now known to have a 'ski-jump' flight deck (an upturned bow end of the flight deck, designed for more efficient operation of STOL{short take-off and landing} aircraft) instead of catapults. These facts seem to suggest that the first Soviet nuclear-powered aircraft carrier, which is expected to be completed in the late 1980s, will still operate vertical or short take-off and landing aircraft, whose performance will inevitably be limited, compared to the US Navy's CTOL combat aircraft.

Since 1922, when its first aircraft carrier, the *Langley*, was commissioned, the US Navy has had more than 65 years of experience in developing and operating carrier-borne aircraft systems. The navy has developed several generations of aircraft carriers equipped with powerful and reliable steam catapults and arresting gear, as well as highly sophisticated carrier-borne aircraft. It would be hard for the Soviets to catch up with the US Navy's technology and vast amount of knowledge in this new field of aircraft-carrier operations. The past record of aircraft development also shows that attempts to convert land-based aircraft into carrier-borne aircraft have ended either in total failure or at best with unsatisfactory results.

Another major problem for the Soviet aircraft-carrier programme would be the development of small airborne early warning (AEW) aircraft, without which no fleet can detect low-flying hostile aircraft approaching it, ready to launch their lethal 'sea-skimming' anti-ship missiles. The loss of the *HMS Sheffield* and other British ships to Argentine air attacks in the Falklands conflict only reconfirmed the indispensability of AEW aircraft for a fleet air defence.

But the Soviet electronics industry has yet to produce successfully, at least in the form of series production, even large land-based AEW aircraft, which Soviet air defence must desperately need in large numbers. Though it has had Tu-26 (Moss) AEW aircraft since the late 1960s, the small number produced (estimated to be about 15) seems to confirm reports concerning their unsatisfactory look-down capability— the ability to pick up targets from ground reflection of radar waves.

Its successor, the AEW version of the IL-76 transport aircraft, code-named 'Mainstay' by the North Atlantic Treaty Organization (NATO), has been under development since the 1970s. Its slow development and the report that only a few were operational by 1985 might suggest the technological difficulties the Soviets have been facing.[4]

To develop a small, reliable and really effective AEW aircraft fit for carrier-deck launching needs, a higher degree of sophistication in micro-electronics is required. Judging from the fact that even the US Navy suffered seriously from the low reliability of early types of carrier-borne AEW aircraft (the E-2A), it is questionable whether the Soviet Union could ever succeed in the foreseeable future in developing a small AEW aircraft. The usual Soviet design technique of compensating for the lack of sophistication and reliability by making things larger and by duplication of the same type of equipment would not work as far as carrier-borne aircraft are concerned, since their sizes and numbers are limited by hanger deck space. If the Soviet Navy uses helicopters for AEW purposes aboard future aircraft carriers, their capability will be even more limited, because of their inherent short range, the small electronics load and low service altitude.

Table 3. Kiev Class ship construction periods

Ship	Laid down	Commissioned	Construction period
Kiev	Sep. 1970	May 1975	4 years, 8 months
Minsk	Dec. 1972	Feb. 1978	5 years, 2 months
Novorossiysk	Sep. 1975	Aug. 1982	7 years
Baku	Dec. 1978	1987	more than 8 years

Conceivable reasons for delays:
1. Skepticism towards the capability of this class.
2. Afghanistan War costs.
3. Priority controversies between navy and other services.

New Soviet aircraft carrier

Displacement:	65 000 tons
Propulsion:	nuclear, and possibly reheat
No catapult:	has a ski-jump flight deck

(Possibly going to embark STOL variant of Forger)

Problems:
1. Lack of high-power steam catapults.
2. Lack of carrier-borne fighter/attacker.
3. Lack of small airborne early warning aircraft.
4. At least several CVs will be needed to cope with 15 US CVs.

Moreover, if the Soviet Union were to challenge US dominance of the sea's surface, it would have to build at least several regular aircraft carriers and concentrate them either in the Atlantic or the Pacific. Otherwise they would be overwhelmed by the 15 aircraft carrier force of the US Navy, and in wartime they would have to hide in ports or in coastal waters like other surface ships. But in view of the Soviet Union's economic constraints; its necessity to maintain a large army and an air force, if only to guard its long borders and secure its position in Eastern Europe; and considering the low status of its navy in the military hierarchy, it is very doubtful that such priority in budget allocation is or will be given to aircraft carriers.

The curiously slow pace of constructing later Kiev Class carriers seems to suggest budgetary difficulties or controversies overshadowing Admiral Gorshkov's aircraft carrier programme. That is, the first ship, the *Kiev*, as commissioned four years and eight months after its keel was laid. The second ship, the *Minsk*, took more than five years. The third, the *Novorossiysk*, took seven years. And the fourth ship, said to be named *Baku*, whose construction started in December 1978, also in the Nikolayev South shipyard on the Black Sea coast, had not come out to the Mediterranean as of early 1988, more than nine years since her construction began (see table 3). Since it is usual that the first ship of a class needs more time to build than later ones, the reason for this abnormal delay is probably politico-financial rather than technological.

That Admiral Gorshkov was relieved in December 1985, without fanfare, his position being succeeded by Admiral V. N. Chernavin, a nuclear submarine officer, might suggest that the Soviet leadership is going to steer its navy into a more rational, although less spectacular, course which puts more emphasis upon submarines and land-based naval aircraft than large surface ships that can serve more for self-satisfaction or national vanity than real national security needs.

Surface ships

In surface ships, too, the USA and its allied navies have obvious advantages over the Soviet Navy and its allies. The Soviet Navy has about 315 major surface combatants (aircraft carriers, cruisers, destroyers and frigates, including KGB border patrol frigates, equivalent to US Coast Guard 'cutters'). Plus, its allies in the Warsaw Pact have in total 10 destroyers and frigates.

The US Navy has 281 major surface combatants, including those in refit or used for reserve personnel training (this includes the 9 most modern Perry Class frigates completed in the 1980s). The US naval allies in NATO and in the Pacific have 303 major surface combatants (UK 56 ships, Japan 51, Italy 29, Canada 23, Republic of Korea 21, Greece 20, Turkey 18, Portugal 17, Federal Republic of Germany 16, Netherlands 15, Australia 12, Denmark 10, Norway 7, Belgium 4, New Zealand 4). In addition to this, France (46 ships) and Spain (28 ships), which are NATO members, although not members of its integrated military organization, should be taken into account. Some Latin

American countries which have mutual defence agreements with the USA through the Treaty of Rio have sizeable navies, such as those of Argentina (12 surface ships), and Brazil (17 ships), among others. To summarize these figures, it could be said that the United States and its allies have about twice as many major surface combatants as the Soviet Union and its allies (see table 4).

Table 4. Comparison of US-allied and Soviet-allied major surface combatants

USA and allies		USSR and allies	
USA	281 (including reserve)	USSR	315
UK	56	Romania	4
Italy	29	GDR	3
Canada	23	Bulgaria	3
Greece	20	*Total*	*325*
Turkey	18		
Portugal	17		
FRG	16		
Netherlands	15		
Denmark	10		
Norway	7		
Belgium	4		
	496		
France	46		
Spain	28		
	74		
Japan	51		
Republic of Korea	21		
Australia	12		
New Zealand	4		
	88		
Total	*658*		

Table 5. Soviet major surface combatants estimated to be retired by the year 2000

Type	Number	Construction period
Cruisers		
Moskva	2	1967-68
Kresta II	2	1969-77 (total 10 ships built)
Kresta I	4	1967-69
Kynda	4	1962-65
Sverdlov	12	1951-56
Destroyers		
Kashin	15	1963-72 (total 19 ships built)
Kildin		1957-58
SAM Kotlin	8	1954-56
Skoryy	6	1949-54
Frigates		
Grisha I	~5	1968- (total 60 built by 1986)
Mirka	18	1964-67
Riga	45	1952-59
Petya	40	1960-70
	~187	

This numerical difference will further widen towards the end of this century, as the Soviet Navy faces the block retirement of a large number of ships built in the 1950s and 1960s. At present, the Soviet naval inventory includes about 187 major surface combatants (see table 5) which will exceed 30 years of normal service life by the year 2000. But recent Soviet naval surface shipbuilding has been at the rate of four to eight ships per year (see table 6), including two KGB border patrol ships (one Krivak III and one Grisha II per year). This sharp drop in the rate of surface ship construction can be partly attributed to the increased sizes and sophistication of each ship which naturally results in a higher unit cost.

Table 6. **Inventory of new type Soviet surface ships**

Type	1982	1983	1984	1985	1986
Kiev (CV)	3	3	3	4	4
Kirov (CGN)	1	1	2	2	2
Slava (CG)	0	1	1	1	1
Sovremennyy (DDG)	2	2	3	4	5
Udaloy (DDG)	2	2	4	5	7
Krivak (FFG)[a]	32	32	33	33	34
Grisha (FF)[a]	49	52	55	58	60
New completion[b]		4	8	6	6

[a]Including KGB border patrol ships.

[b]Average construction pace: six ships per year.

Source: *Jane's Fighting Ships* (1982-83—1986-87).

Assuming that the Soviet Navy continues to commission new surface ships at the rate of 6 ships per year, the Soviet surface fleet at the end of this century would have about 200 ships, which is 100 less than its present strength. Compared to this, the US Navy plans to have 242 major surface ships, including 4 battleships, by the early part of the 1990s as a part of its 600-ship navy programme.

In view of the serious financial situation of the USA, it is questionable whether or not it can maintain a 600-ship strength level through the 1990s and into the 2000s. None the less, at least the US Navy has the advantage that its major surface combatants are now generally newer than those of the Soviet Navy. The US Navy's list of active ships includes less than 80 ships which were built before 1970. In January 1987, it was building 13 Ticonderoga Class cruisers and 1 Arleigh Burke Class destroyer, both equipped with highly advanced AEGIS anti-air systems. Its shipbuilding programme from 1988 through 1992 includes another 5 Ticonderoga Class and 20 Arleigh Burke Class ships.

If the US Government provides funds for building 5 surface combatants per year through the early part of the 1990s, the US Navy will maintain about 200 major surface combatants in the year 2000, allowing it to have some numerical edge against the Soviet surface fleet by itself without taking US allies into account.

The fleets of the US allies in NATO and the Pacific today include about 190 surface ships built before 1970, which have to be retired by the year 2000. The current shipbuilding pace of these navies will apparently make it difficult to replace all of their ageing ships, and a considerable drop in numbers, perhaps 70 or more, can be anticipated by the end of this century.

Exceptions among Western European navies are those of the Netherlands and Italy. Even within the framework of the present programme, the Dutch Navy will increase by 5 surface combatants and the Italian Navy will have 2 more. In the Pacific, Japan's 'Maritime Self-Defence Force' is going to increase its fleet of major surface combatants from its present 52 ships to 62 by around the year 1994 under the current programme, making it the second largest surface fleet in the non-communist world. It will perhaps exceed 70 by the year 2000 and become par with the Soviet surface fleet in the Pacific.

Although Japan's security arrangements with the United States guarantee that Japan will enter a war only when Japan is attacked, the existence of two major US naval and four US air bases in Japan almost preclude the possibility of its staying out of any major US-Soviet military conflict. Moreover, considering that Japan has been the most active partner in naval joint exercises with the US Navy in the Pacific and that it has joint defence plans with the USA, the Japanese 'Maritime Self-Defence Force' has to be regarded as a US allied navy in any practical sense.

Navy aviation and fleet air defence

In view of the apparent disparity in aircraft carrier strength and the resulting vulnerability of the Soviet surface fleet to US aircraft carrier battle groups, the Soviet Navy still has to rely mainly on its shore-based naval aviation and its submarines to cope with superior US surface fleets. In spite of the Soviet naval buildup, this situation basically has not changed since the 1950s.

Soviet Naval Aviation (SNA) has been large in size since World War II, during which it played a more active role than any other type of

Soviet naval force. Although its fighters were transferred to the PVO (air defence force), it has been equipped with great numbers of jet strike planes, such as the Il-28 (Beagle) twin-jet light bomber and the Tu-16 (Badger) twin-jet medium bomber.

Currently it is believed to have some 900 combat aircraft and 300 anti-submarine helicopters, including 120 Tu-22Ms (Backfire) supersonic bombers and 240 Tu-16s (Badgers) intended for anti-ship attacks. Tu-22Ms can carry one AS-4 (Kitchen; 220 km range) or two AS-6s (Kingfish; 650 km range) air-to-surface missiles (ASMs) and are regarded as the most serious threat to US surface ships and those of its allies. Both missiles are capable of carrying nuclear warheads.

The general air defence plan for US aircraft carrier battle groups is to detect approaching adversary aircraft and intercept them before they can launch their missiles. This is accomplished using the combination of E-2C AEW aircraft for detection and F-14 fighter aircraft armed with long-range Phoenix air-to-air missiles (AAMs) for interception. However, one aircraft carrier cannot keep even one of its four E-2Cs permanently airborne while operating within the estimated 3700-km combat radius of Soviet Backfire bombers. In order to counter the Soviet air threat, the US Navy is going to take such measures as: *(a)* installing over-the-horizon (OTH) radars with a detection range of 3000 km to cover the North Atlantic, western Pacific, Mediterranean and Persian Gulf areas (although OTH radars are less precise and much less reliable than conventional line-of-sight radars, because they rely on ionospheric reflection of high-frequency {HF} signals, they would provide some prior warning to US Fleets about approaching aircraft); *(b)* laying more stress on multiple aircraft carrier operations in one area, to enable at least one E-2C to be kept airborne at all times; *(c)* increasing the number of E-2C from the present four per carrier to five; *(d)* constructing Ticonderoga Class anti-air cruisers and Arleigh Burke Class destroyers equipped with the AEGIS air defence system which can direct 14-to-18 Standard 2MR missiles (range: 150 km) almost simultaneously to different air targets such as anti-ship missiles. At present the US Navy plans to build 27 Ticonderoga Class (9530 t, full load), 29 Arleigh Burke Class (8300 t, full load) and 31 improved versions of the latter type. A future aircraft carrier battle group, centred around 2 aircraft carriers, will include 3 Ticonderoga Class and 4 Arleigh Burke Class ships. The AEGIS air defence system would enable US Fleets to guard themselves fairly effectively against mass attacks by anti-ship missiles.

The US Navy's increased interest in anti-air-warfare (AAW) in recent years reflects its forward strategy, in which it aims at operating closer to the Soviet coast, destroying the Soviet surface fleet and air bases, and conducting anti-submarine operations against Soviet SSBNs (strategic missile-carrying nuclear submarines) in Soviet home waters, such as the Barents Sea and the Sea of Okhotsk. In these areas US Fleets would have to face fierce and intensified counter-attacks by Soviet shore-based airpower.

It is notable that the Soviet Navy Backfire bombers stationed at such bases as Byhkov in Belorussia and Alekseyevka in the Far East do not frequently come out to the Atlantic or the Pacific. For example, in spite of the fact that some 40 Backfires are reportedly based at Alekseyevka on the west coast of the Tartar Strait north of Japan, Japan's Air Self-Defence Force has observed them to fly in groups over the Sea of Japan only twice in the five years from 1982 to 1986 (10 Backfires on 14 September 1982 and 12 on 23 September 1984).[5] Although Soviet Navy bombers are apparently doing more training closer to its coast and in the Sea of Okhotsk, Backfires have never appeared in the Pacific Ocean east of the Japanese archipelago. Only once or twice a year do TU-95 Bear turbo-prop bombers (used for electronic intelligence-gathering) fly long-range reconnaissance missions around Japan.

This training pattern seems to suggest that the strike units of Soviet Naval Aviation are primarily committed to attacks against US Fleets that approach close to the Soviet coast in such areas as the Norwegian Sea, or off the coast of the Kamchatka Peninsula and the Kuril Islands, rather than attacking US Fleets or its allied shipping in remote parts of the oceans, in spite of the long-range capabilities of SNA aircraft. Thus, lacking in experience and daily training for long-range oceanic navigation in peacetime, it should be doubted whether or not Soviet bomber crews can perform well in locating, identifying and attacking a fleet of merchant or naval ships in the open sea, a thousand kilometres away from its coast, in wartime situations.

III. Submarines (and anti-submarine warfare)

Introduction

The US Navy has had, and probably will continue to have, over-whelming superiority in sea-based airpower. This superiority, coupled with the powerful surface fleets of the United States and its allies, would guarantee Western dominance of the ocean's surface for the foreseeable future. Since the 1950s, however, the Soviet Union has been building up a large submarine fleet in an attempt to counter Western sea control.

Traditionally, submarines have served weak navies as favourable weapons with the aim of challenging strong opponents. Most major submarine developments have always come from the USA, ever since David Bushwell first invented a man-powered submarine and used it to attack British men-of-war blockading New York harbour during the War for American Independence. Robert Fulton then built a workable steam-propelled submarine, and John P. Holland developed the first modern submarine with an internal combustion engine, an electric motor, and armed with torpedoes. And it was, of course, the US Navy's Admiral Hyman Rickover who led the development of the first nuclear-powered submarine, the *USS Nautilus*. It is thus ironic that the US Navy today is in a similar position to that of the British Navy during the nineteenth century in that it has a global command of the sea and regards submarines as its greatest threat.

The submarine proved to be a formidable weapon already in World War I. In World War II, German U-boats sank as many as 2700 ships and again brought Britain to the brink of economic collapse. In the Pacific, US submarines caused the loss of 1400 Japanese ships and became the single most important factor for Japan's surrender.

The introduction of nuclear propulsion and nuclear weaponry aboard submarines in the late 1950s revolutionized the capability and destructive power of submarines. A conventionally powered (diesel on surface, electric motor underwater) submarine has to surface (at the very latest, after about 48 hours of underwater operation at low speed) to get fresh air for its crew and to recharge batteries by starting the diesel engines. And if it operates at a maximum speed of about 20 knots (modern conventional submarines), the batteries will be almost totally discharged within 30 minutes.

Nuclear-powered submarines, however, can operate underwater continuously for two months or more, in other words, as long as food and other supplies or the crew's endurance can last.

Also, whereas World War II submarines were armed with deck guns and torpedoes that had an effective range of several kilometres and had a warhead containing several hundred kilograms of explosives, current strategic submarines can carry up to 24 intercontinental-range (approximately 8000 km) missiles, each carrying as many as 8 or more thermonuclear warheads with a destructive power comparable to 100 000 tons of high explosives.

Even when the strategic nuclear force aspects are put aside (see chapter 3), the implications of submarine forces in the East-West conventional military balance are preponderant because of the following factors:

1. If the anti-submarine warfare (ASW) forces of the West were unable to cope with Soviet submarines, either numerically or technologically, then Western superiority in aircraft carriers and surface ships would lose its value. For example, should submarine technology develop so radically in the future *vis-à-vis* anti-submarine technology that the surface ship would become indefensible against submarines, then aircraft carriers and other ships would have to stay in harbours, surrendering sea control to submarines. (This actually happened to the Argentine aircraft carrier, *Veintecinco de Mayo*, during the Falklands conflict in 1983. A few British nuclear submarines that patrolled off the coast deterred it from leaving the Buenos Aires port.)

2. In case of ground warfare in Europe and Korea, US and its allied strategies call for large supplies and reinforcements to be sent from the continental United States. Should war break out in Europe, it is assumed that at least 1244 transport ships would be required to sail across the Atlantic, carrying reinforcements, equipment and supplies from North America to Europe, including 1.5-million military personnel, *matériel* for 90 air force squadrons and 4.5-million tons of ammunition.[6] These cargo ships are more vulnerable targets to submarine attacks than warships because they are so numerous and usually cannot be as densely escorted as 'high value' warships, like aircraft carriers. But whether or not US and its allied army troops and air force units in Western Europe could be adequately supplied and reinforced would be as important for the defence of Western Europe as the numbers of US soldiers or air force squadrons already stationed in Western Europe.

3. The economic systems of the non-Soviet bloc nations are based upon free sea traffic. Most industrialized nations rely heavily on imported food, raw materials and fuel; and depend upon sea transport for their economic viability. In 1983, 1169-million tons of goods were unloaded, in international sea-borne traffic, at the ports of 13 NATO member nations in Europe, including Turkey. Three hundred and ninety-five million tons were unloaded at US and Canadian ports. Japan imported 550-million tons of goods in the same year.[7] If sea

routes of commerce were disrupted by submarines, it would be a serious blow to the Western industrialized nations, as well as to many other nations whose economies rely upon exports and imports.

These factors apply to the Soviet Union and its allies only to a small degree because they are connected by land traffic. The total tonnage of goods unloaded in the Soviet Union and its four Warsaw Treaty Organization (WTO) allies on the Baltic and Black Seas (the GDR, Poland, Romania and Bulgaria) in 1983 was 213-million tons, which was less than one-seventh of that of the 15 seafaring NATO nations.[8] The Soviet bloc's military supplies, reinforcements and civilian products can be transported by railways, motor vehicles, pipelines and river craft. (The only major exception for the Soviet Union is its Pacific coast. Because of the total lack of railroads and highways to connect the Kamchatka Peninsula to the rest of Soviet territory, the supplies to its major naval port at Petropavlovsk-Kamchatskiy on the east coast of the peninsula have to be transported by ships from the Vladivostok area.)

Although land transportation is generally more expensive and less efficient than sea traffic for long distance and large bulk transport, its relative redundancy and resiliency in wartime is one obvious strategic advantage for the Soviets and their allies. While Western navies have to control the sea and defend a large amount of shipping, the Soviet Navy can concentrate on 'sea denial' missions aimed at disrupting Western use of the sea. This asymmetrical strategic condition is one important factor to be taken into consideration in discussing the naval arms race and naval arms control.

Soviet and US submarine forces

In its submarine force, the Soviet Navy has at least numerical superiority to the US Navy. In 1986 the Soviet Navy was believed to have 364 submarines,[9] out of which 186 were nuclear-powered. These submarines consisted of 76 ballistic missile submarines (62 were nuclear-powered), 67 anti-ship missile submarines (50 were nuclear-powered) and 218 torpedo-carrying attack submarines (73 were nuclear-powered). Among its WTO allies, only Poland and Bulgaria have 3 obsolete submarines each.

The US Navy has 139 submarines, consisting of 38 ballistic missile submarines (all nuclear-powered), 97 nuclear-powered attack submarines carrying torpedoes, anti-submarine nuclear missiles (SUB-ROC), anti-ship missiles (Harpoon) and cruise missiles (Tomahawk). Only 4 conventionally powered submarines remain.

The other NATO countries have 121 submarines altogether, including the UK's 18 nuclear-powered and 15 conventionally powered submarines, France's 10 nuclear-powered and 14 conventionally powered submarines, and Spain's 8 conventionally powered submarines. US allies in the Pacific have 20 conventionally powered submarines (Japan 14, Australia 6) and US allies in Latin America in all have 34 conventionally powered submarines. If all these are combined, it can be said that the US Navy and its allied navies have 346 submarines in total compared to the 370 of the Soviet Union and its allies (see table 7). However, whereas 364 Soviet submarines can operate under the single national command and with the same operational concepts, submarines of US allies are designed to meet each nation's purposes. Especially submarines of Latin American navies cannot be expected to take part in naval conflicts in the northern hemisphere, although many of them are fairly modern submarines of West German design.

Since the emergence of submarine-launched strategic missiles, submarines have been divided into two categories: strategic or ballistic missile submarines; and attack submarines, which are intended for attacking surface ships and submarines. In the Soviet case, the latter category of submarines could be divided into another two categories: anti-ship missile submarines, and other attack submarines armed with torpedoes and anti-submarine missiles. Also, submarines are separated by propulsion systems into nuclear-powered submarines and conventionally powered ones, which use diesel engines and electric batteries.

The combinations of these factors have made six categories of submarines: *(a)* nuclear-powered ballistic missile submarines (SSBNs); *(b)* conventionally powered ballistic missile submarines (SSBs); *(c)* nuclear-powered cruise missile submarines (SSGNs); *(d)* conventionally powered cruise missile submarines (SSGs); *(e)* nuclear-powered attack submarines (SSNs); and *(f)* conventionally powered attack submarines (SSs).

With the introduction of cruise missiles which can be launched from torpedo tubes against ships and land targets, such as the US Tomahawk missile which has a 2500-km range and a 5 to 150-kt nuclear warhead (nuclear land-attack version), or its Soviet equivalent, the SS-N-21, the

Table 7. Comparison of US-allied and Soviet-allied submarine forces

USA and allies[a]	Number	USSR and allies	Number
USA	139	USSR	364
UK	33	Poland	3
FRG	24	Bulgaria	3
Turkey	16	*Total*	*370*
Norway	14		
Italy	10		
Greece	10		
Netherlands	4		
Denmark	4		
Portugal	3		
Canada	3		
	260		
France	24		
Spain	8		
	32		
Japan	14		
Australia	6		
	20		
Total	*312*		

[a] US allies in Latin America have 34 submarines.

Source: *Jane's Fighting Ships* (1986-87).

distinctions between strategic missile submarines, anti-ship missile submarines and attack submarines are becoming somewhat blurred. But since some distinction still remains between strategic (ballistic missile) submarines and submarines with primarily anti-ship/submarine roles, comparisons and discussions of submarine forces will be made according to such categories.

Strategic submarines

Although the strategic submarine forces of all nuclear weapon nations are discussed in chapter 3, several comparative points concerning Soviet and US submarines are important to make here.

Even though the Soviet Navy was the first to build ballistic missile submarines, it had long suffered from technological gaps. It had converted Zulu Class conventional submarines to carry two SSN-N-4 missiles (range: 480 km) in the 1955-57 period. (The first US ballistic missile nuclear-powered submarine, *George Washington*, was completed in 1960.) The first of the Yankee Class submarines, which was completed in 1967, can be regarded as equivalent to the first US SSBNs—the George Washington Class—deployed in 1960. But one major difference was that the SS-N-6 missiles on the Yankee Class had to use liquid fuel (such as dinitrogen tetraoxide {N2O4} plus unsymmetric dimethyl hydrazine) which requires a great deal of maintenance and is dangerous to carry in cramped and unventilated submarine spaces. This problem was evidenced by the fire and explosion in a missile tube aboard one of the Yankees off of Bermuda in October 1986. The accident caused the submarine to sink.[10] Since 1960, however, US Polaris submarine-launched ballistic missiles (SLBMs) used more stable and almost carefree solid propellants.

Another problem of the Yankee Class submarines was that they had to approach relatively close to the US coast in order to cover inland targets with their 3000-km range missiles. In so doing, they exposed themselves to the growing US anti-submarine forces by transiting through the Greenland-Iceland-UK (GIUK) gap and also by patrolling areas off the US Atlantic and Pacific coasts.

The Soviet Union solved the latter problem in 1972 with the deployment of Delta I Class submarines carrying 12 intercontinental range missiles, which enabled them to deliver nuclear strikes at their targets in the US mainland directly from Soviet home waters. But they too had to use liquid fuel, and as most Soviet ICBMs, many Soviet SLBMs use it even today.

The operational rate of storable liquid-fuelled missiles has to be generally much lower than solid-fuelled missiles because the former need more frequent checks of fuel and oxidizer tanks, piping, valves and seals. Some of these parts have to be exchanged regularly. Probably every time such a check is made, tanks will have to be emptied and refilled with volatile liquids. In spite of the obvious advantages of solid fuel as the propellant of military rockets, as well as the fact that US Polaris SLBMs have had solid fuel since 1960, the Soviet Union has kept producing liquid-fuelled ICBMs and SLBMs. Though the new Soviet mobile ICBMs (the SS-24 and the SS-25) are believed to have solid fuel, the Soviets are still developing a new liquid-fuelled SLBM (the SS-N-23) carried by the Delta IV Class submarines.

Solid-fuelled long-range missiles will need such technologies as: *(a)* a propellant with a high thrust/weight ratio to achieve long range and adequate payload; *(b)* a highly homogenized composition of propellant which can guarantee stable burning; *(c)* thrust control mechanisms which are more complex than liquid fuel systems using valves; and *(d)* lighter warheads to be carried by solid rockets which generally have less thrust.

The success of Polaris was made possible because US technologies in the 1950s could achieve technological breakthroughs in these areas. But Soviet attempts to produce solid-fuelled ICBMs were not successful at least until the latter half of the 1980s. Only some 60 solid-fuelled SS-13 ICBMs were produced starting in the late 1960s, and they are known to have very poor accuracy.[11] Their apparent successor (the SS-16) which was tested in the 1970s, was probably a failure, as none were deployed operationally.

The Delta II and III submarines increased the number of missiles to 16 per submarine, and the payload of each missile was also increased. But the liquid-fuelled SS-N-18 missiles carried by Delta IIIs have either a long range with one warhead (Mod {modification} 2) or a reduced range with multiple warheads (Mod I or 3).

The Typhoon Class, the first of which was completed in 1981, seems at least theoretically to suggest that the Soviet Union has solved these problems. Its 20 SS-N-20 missiles are believed to have solid propellant, long-range and multiple independently targeted re-entry warheads, though this new missile apparently had difficulties in the testing stage. But, the trade-off was the Typhoon's immense size of 25 000 t, with 80 000 shaft horsepower (shp) from two nuclear power plants, and a bulky hull (two pressure hulls are combined horizontally like a double-barrelled shotgun and covered with one outer hull). This type would be slower, less manoeuvrable and easier to detect for attack submarines than the sleek 18 700 ton US Ohio Class strategic missile submarines with a 60 000 shp engine. Although the Typhoon has attracted much attention because of its enormous size (at first, the Typhoon was estimated to be 30 000 t), it being the largest submarine ever built, comparing it with the US Ohio Class submarine would show that its size reflects the weaker Soviet technological level rather than its real strength, just as the 'largest watch or tape recorder in the world' is not necessarily the best. Additionally, there is the issue of hull design. Some Soviet submarines, including the Typhoon Class, have a 'double hull' design—one or more inner pressure hulls and an outer hull. Soviet double hull submarine design has been cited as a special feature and advantage of such classes because it is believed to be less vulnerable to damage or destruction by conventional torpedoes than are single hull designs. But double hulls have been more traditional to submarine design since before World War I, since submarines need inter-hull space to fill with air in order to provide buoyancy. So foreign observers are claiming that the backwardness of Soviet technology is the new technology.

US strategic missile submarines consist of basically two types: those carrying Poseidon (C3) missiles and those carrying Trident I (C4) missiles. There are currently 36 such submarines equipped with some 640 SLBMs and more than 5600 nuclear warheads.

One major factor that guarantees US superiority in submarine-based strategic nuclear force is the high operational rate of US submarines. Even old Lafayette Class submarines have been deployed to sea 55 per cent of the time, and with the Ohio Class the figure rose to about 66 per cent. The latter conduct 70-day patrols interrupted by crew change-over and replenishment periods lasting for 25 days. After nine years of service they will have a 12-month major overhaul when recoring of the nuclear reactor and modifications, such as fitting of new type missiles, will be done.[12]

This high 'at-sea to in-port' ratio of US strategic missile submarines is enabled by the fact that each submarine has two crews ('Blue' and 'Gold') assigned. The sea deployment rate of Soviet strategic missile submarines is reported to be from 11 to 15 per cent, with usually about eight ballistic missile submarines on patrol.

Thus the US Navy, with half the number of ballistic missile submarines that the Soviet Navy has, deploys at any time 20 or more submarines carrying more than 3800 warheads on station compared to about 8 Soviet submarines at sea carrying perhaps less than 500 warheads, although during a crisis the Soviet Union could send more submarines to sea for a limited period even if they have only one crew per submarine.

These factors, combined with the lack of Soviet capability to conduct ASW on a global scale, make US superiority in the category of

SLBMs almost unquestionable, and a means by which the United States can mostly compensate for any theoretical or numerical inferiority in land-based ICBMs. There can be no doubt about the increasing importance of strategic submarine forces. As the accuracy of strategic missiles is increased and targeting systems improved, the fixed land-based ICBMs of both sides become more vulnerable to pre-emptive strikes, even though some ICBMs will become land-mobile. The SLBMs, which are much less vulnerable to first strikes and which are rapidly increasing in accuracy, will become more preponderant in the nuclear force structure. The USA, which has three times as many strategic warheads aboard submarines as on ICBMs—6300 compared with 2110—will then have the advantages brought forth by this trend in technological developments.

Attack submarines

With its attack submarine force (anti-ship/anti-submarine), however, the USA does not necessarily enjoy such clear advantage because of the asymmetric strategic conditions that require the US Navy to protect its shipping and the large number of Soviet submarines with which the USA and its allies have to cope. In view of the fact that in 1939 57 U-boats of the German Navy could seriously threaten the British economy, the Soviet's 286 submarines with anti-ship/anti-submarine attack roles could cause fatal damage to Western shipping if no adequate countermeasures are provided. Of these 286 attack submarines, 124 are nuclear-powered and 67 of them are armed with anti-ship missiles and, naturally, the capabilities of these 286 submarines have grown beyond comparison with the submarines of World War II.

Submarines specially designed to carry anti-ship missiles are characteristic to the Soviet Navy. Although submarines of other navies can carry anti-ship missiles, those missiles can be launched from torpedo tubes and do not need special submarines. Since the 1950s the Soviet Navy has armed its submarines, as well as its surface ships, with a wide variety of anti-ship missiles in an attempt to have some weapon system to counter US aircraft carrier groups. But the large size of these missiles still requires that special submarines be built to carry them. For example, Soviet SS-N-12 anti-ship missiles (estimated range: 550 km) carried aboard Slava Class cruisers and Kirov Class aircraft carriers have an estimated length of 11.7 m (as big as a jet fighter) and a huge diameter, while the US Tomahawk cruise missile (range: 450-2500 km) is 6.4 m long and has a diameter of 53 cm. The SS-N-19 missile of the new Soviet anti-ship-missile submarines, which is a modification of the SS-N-12, would not be much smaller. Also the Soviet's SS-N-9 missile (range: 110 km; warhead: 225 kg) is 8.8 m long and weighs more than 4 tons, while the US Harpoon (range: 110 km; warhead: 225 kg), is 4.5 m long and 680 kg in weight. These large Soviet missile sizes seem to suggest a wide technological gap in sensors, computers and propulsion systems. The principle types of Soviet anti-ship missile submarine as of 1986 are shown in table 8.

Table 8. Principal Soviet anti-ship submarines—1986

Number & class of submarine	Displacement (tons)	Number & type of ASM	Number of torpedo tubes	Speed (knots)	Comments
3 Oscar	16000	24 SS-N-19	6	33	nuclear-powered; more being built
6 Charlie II	5500	8 SS-N-9	6	24	nuclear-powered
11 Charlie I	4800	8 SS-N-7	6	24	nuclear-powered
29 Echo II	6200	8 SS-N-3 or SS-N-12	8	24	nuclear-powered; built in 1960s; becoming obsolete
16 Juliett	4300	4 SS-N-3	6	12	conventionally powered

The SS-N-7 missile, carried by Charlie I submarines, and its modification, the SS-N-9 of Charlie IIs, are designed for submerged launching and have an estimated range of 60 km and 110 km, respectively. These missiles are capable of being launched from outside of the anti-submarine screen of destroyers and frigates around aircraft carriers. In this range, Charlies can acquire general positions of surface ships (by listening to their noises through passive sonars) and launch their missiles while submerged. In order to counter these submarine-launched missiles with anti-air-missiles and rapid-firing machine guns, opponent fleets have to keep radar-equipped aircraft, including heli-copters constantly in the air to provide early warning. But long-range anti-ship missiles, such as the SS-N-19 carried by the Oscar or the SS N-12 and the old SS-N-3, need extra target acquisition means because it is evident that a submarine cannot know the exact location and identity of surface ships 500 km away. Therefore either an aircraft or a surveillance satellite should first locate the target and then the information has to be conveyed to the submarine. In order to receive the necessary data, such as the opponent ship's position, heading, speed, plus wind direction and wind speed, submarines have either to keep their antennas on the surface, or rely on extra/very low frequency (ELF/VLF) communication. This latter type of communication can be received underwater but only extremely slowly, and it does not work for the transmission of complicated messages, such as targeting data. The existence of an ELF/VLF buoy in Oscar Class submarines seems to suggest that at least initially ELF/VLF is used possibly to instruct them to bring their antennas to surface. If Soviet submarines have to extend their antennas above the surface to obtain targeting data from external sources, adversary anti-submarine aircraft will have some chance to find and destroy them before they can launch their missiles. And if they cannot, US aircraft carrier battle groups could cope with the anti-ship missiles with their AEGIS (an advanced air defence system) and other anti-air warfare weapon systems.

Because SS-N-3 missiles carried by 12 conventionally powered Julietts and some nuclear-powered Echo IIs were originally developed for surface ships, submarines carrying these have to surface before launching, thus very much limiting their value.

The Soviet Navy has had the world's largest submarine fleet since the 1930s. And as mentioned before, 1200 submarines were planned to be built in Stalin's era for coastal defence. Moreover, although this programme was suspended because of the construction of the first nuclear submarine, the *USS Nautilus*, completed in 1954, the Soviet Navy soon followed the US lead by building 13 nuclear-powered November Class SSNs. The first of the November Class SSNs was completed in 1958. However, these submarines are extremely noisy and easily detected.

The Soviet Navy then built the Victor I, II and III series from 1969 to 1985. These have advanced 'tear drop' type hulls, but still have many free-flood holes that must make noise and are also somewhat slower than US attack submarines, although the last version—Victor III—showed much improvement in noise-suppressing technology. Forty-four Victors carrying torpedoes and SS-N-15/16 anti-submarine missiles (in Victor II and III) constitute the mainstay of Soviet anti-submarine submarines, which they need if only to protect their SSBNs from US attack submarines.

Six Alfa Class submarines have more than a 42-knot maximum speed, reportedly with a liquid metal-cooled nuclear propulsion reactor, and possibly with a titanium hull. It is said that these submarines have a 750-m diving depth, although at this speed their sonars would be masked by their own noises, making it easy for opponents to locate them. Their high speed and remarkable diving depth might make present Western anti-submarine torpedoes almost ineffective (MK-46 torpedo, widely used by Western navies, has a maximum speed of 46 knots). After the construction of Alfa stopped in 1983, the Soviet Navy commissioned three new types of nuclear attack submarine—the Sierra, Mike and Akula Classes appeared almost simultaneously between 1984 and 1985—and the construction of second boats of the Sierra and Akula Classes were still in progress in 1986. Compared with the production rate of Victor III (21 of which were completed in the eight years between 1978 and 1985), the slow pace at which these new types are being built is notable. Besides the Sierra and Akula Classes, the Soviet Union is building Typhoon, Delta IV (SSBNs), Oscar (SSGNs) and Kilo Class conventionally powered attack submarines; whereas the United States is building only two types: the Ohio Class (SSBNs) and the Los Angeles Class (SSNs). It should be noted that the US Los Angeles Class submarines are being constructed at a pace of four boats per year.

Building so many types of submarine simultaneously would generally complicate the problems of production, maintenance, supply and training. But the reason that the Soviet Navy does this might be that they need successors to various types of submarine which they already have for different purposes. Another reason could be that Soviet submarine designers have yet to succeed in producing a satisfactory type of general-purpose submarine that can perform various missions, such as anti-submarine, anti-aircraft carrier, cruise missile land attack, coastal defence, and so on. In contrast, the US Los Angeles Class can perform various roles with one type, carrying a variety of weapons and various fire control systems. US attack submarines can carry such weapons as the MK-48 anti-submarine/surface ship torpedo, SUBROC (and later the anti-submarine warfare stand-off weapon {ASW/SOW}; rocket-propelled torpedo or nuclear-depth charge), Harpoon anti-ship and land-attack missiles, Tomahawk long-range cruise missiles, and mines, including self-propelled ones like the MK-67.

The only type of submarine that three Soviet shipyards are building in large numbers today is the Kilo Class conventionally powered submarine (some of which are for export). However, the completion of 10 Kilos in seven years from 1980 to 1986 (recently 3 per year) is nothing compared with the staggering production pace of about 70 Soviet submarines commissioned per year in the late 1950s. While the USA is not building any diesel-electric-powered submarines, the fact that the Soviet Union is building large numbers of these less expensive submarines for coastal defence is because they have to fill the gap that will be made by the forthcoming retirement of the ageing fleet of 60 Foxtrot Class and other diesel-electric-powered submarines.

Today, it is generally believed that the Soviet Navy has about 364 submarines. But this large submarine fleet includes about 80 boats that belong to the Whiskey, Romeo, Zulu and Golf Classes which were built mostly in the 1950s. A submarine's normal service life is 30 years or less, even with extremely good maintenance and some modifications. It is remarkable that at least some of these boats, based on World War II German U-boat design concepts, are still being operated by the Soviet Navy. Also about 50 first-generation nuclear submarines (November; Echo I and II; and Hotel II and III) built from the late 1950s to the 1960s presumably will have to be phased out within several years, along with 60 Foxtrot diesel submarines which seem reliable but by no means modern. Sixteen Juliett diesel-powered anti-ship missile submarines, built in the1960s, also might be retired (or modified for use elsewhere) rather early because of the apparent limitation of its SS-N-3 anti-ship missile system that can be launched only from the surface and also because of its slow speed (12 knots, dived).

By around the end of this century, most of the 33 Yankee Class submarines (completed between 1967 and 1974 and being converted from SSBN to other roles) and some of the 11 Charlie Is (1967-72) and the 16 Victor Is (1967-74) will reach their retirement period. Thus, by around the year 2000, some 240 submarines will have to be retired from the present inventory of about 360 (see table 9).

Table 9. Soviet submarines estimated to be retired by the year 2000

Type	Number	Construction period	Status
Whiskey (SS)	50	1951-57	Being phased out
Romeo (SS)	6	1958-61	"
Zulu (SS)	2	1951-55	"
Golf I, II, III (SSG)	18	1958-62	"
November (SSN)	12	1958-63	Obsolete nuclear
Echo I (SSN)	5	1960-62	boats to be retired
Echo II (SSGN)	29	1961-67	by mid-1990s,
Hotel II, III (SSBN)	7	1958-62	with the exception
			of some Echo IIs
			with new missiles
Foxtrot (SS)	60	1958-71	Diesel boats to be
Juliett (SSG)	16	1961-68	retired by the year 2000
Yankee (SSBN)	33	1967-74	Some of these will
Charlie I (SSGN)	11	1967-72	be retired by the
Victor I (SSN)	7	1968-74	year 2000
Total	*256*		

[a] 230 to 240 of the current 364 submarines will have to be retired by the year 2000.

Information on recent Soviet submarine construction, however, can be obtained from *Jane's Fighting Ships* series, which have annually reported the inventory of Soviet submarines. The new types in each year from 1982 to 1986 are shown in table 10. This table shows that 25 submarines were completed by Soviet shipyards in four years, including 12 diesel-electric-powered boats, from 1983 to 1986, putting the average building rate at 6.25 submarines a year. The present construction pace of the six classes of submarine which were currently being built can be roughly estimated as follows: Typhoon (SSBN)—one every year; Delta IV (SSBN)—one every year; Oscar (SSGN)—one every two years; Sierra (SSN)—one every two years; Akula (SSN)—one every two years; and Kilo (SS)—three every year; or a total of seven or less per year.

Table 10. Inventory of new type Soviet submarines

Type	1982	1983	1984	1985	1986
Typhoon (SSBN)	1	2	2	3	4
Delta IV (SSBN)	0	0	0	1	2
Delta III (SSBN)	13	14	14	14	14
Oscar (SSGN)	1	1	2	2	3
Mike (SSN)	0	0	1	1	1
Sierra (SSN)	0	0	1	1	1
Akula (SSN)	0	0	0	1	1
Alfa (SSN)	5	6	6	6	6
Victor III (SSN)	13	14	14	14	14
Kilo (SS)[a]	1	4	5	5	10
Tango (SS)	15	18	18	18	18
New completion		10	4	3	8

[a] Kilo construction in 1986 includes boats built for export.

Source: *Jane's Fighting Ships* (1982-83—1986-87).

So it would not be wrong to estimate that unless some drastic change occurs, Soviet submarine construction will keep the pace of six to seven boats per year on average, including the Kilo Class, some of which are built for export. (The Indian Navy, which has used eight

Soviet-built Foxtrot Classes has ordered six Kilos and received one in 1986; other navies with old Soviet-built submarines might follow suit.)

Assuming that the Soviet Navy continues to receive about 7 submarines per year, it will have less than 100 new submarines by the year 2000 as the replacement for about 240 submarines to be retired between now and then. Thus it seems possible that the Soviet submarine fleet strength will decrease from the present 370 to about 230 by the end of the century. Even if the building pace were quickened, so that they build five nuclear-powered submarines (one of each type) and 5 Kilos per year excluding those intended for export, the Soviet Navy will still have about 100 less submarines by the year 2000 compared with today's strength.

It should be remembered, however, that the size and capability of each Soviet submarine will increase, for example, to enable them to carry SS-N-21 cruise missiles. Nevertheless, similar qualitative increases will also apply to the US Navy and its allied navies, and this will largely offset the Soviet submarines' qualitative improvements.

If the current submarine construction rate continues, the Soviet active submarine force can be estimated to comprise the following submarines around the year 2000, although this inevitably includes many uncertainties regarding details:

70 SSBNs (18 Typhoon Class, 16 Delta IV Class, 14 Delta III Class, 4 Delta II Class, 18 Delta l Class);
24 SSGNs (10 Oscar Class, 6 Charlie II Class, 8 Charlie I Class);
65 SSNs (16 Sierra/Akula Classes, 6 Alpha Class, 21 Victor II Class, 7 Victor II Class, 15 Victor I Class); and
70 SSs (52 Kilo Class, 18 Tango Class).

The present Soviet attack (anti-ship/anti-submarine) submarine force includes the types presented in table 11. In addition to those, the Soviet Navy has 39 nuclear-powered submarines, such as the Yankee and Hotel Classes, which are former ballistic missile submarines with their missiles removed, and the ageing November Class nuclear-powered submarines. It also has 68 other conventional submarines, most of which are very old.

Table 11. Principal Soviet attack submarine force—1987

Number & class of submarine	Submerged displacement (tons)	Type of missile	Number of torpedo tubes	Speed (knots)	Comments
2 Akula	8000	SS-NX-21[a] (possibly) SS-N-15/16[b]	6	30	nuclear-powered; more being built
1 Mike	9700	SS-NX-21[a] (possibly) SS-NX-15/16[b]	6	35	"
1 Sierra	8000	SS-NX-21[a] (possibly) SS-N-15/16[b]	6	32	"
6 Alfa	3700	SS-N-15[b]	6	42	nuclear-powered; diving depth: 750 metres
21 Victor III	6300	SS-N-21[a] (possibly) SS-N-15/16[b]	6	30	nuclear-powered
7 Victor II	6000	SS-N-15/16[b]	6	29	"
16 Victor I	5300	SS-N-15[b]	6	29	"
10 Kilo	3200	-	8	16	conventionally powered
18 Tango	3900	SS-N-15/16[b] (possibly)	8	16	"
60 Foxtrot	2500	-	6	16	"

[a] These are considered candidate submarines for the SS-N-21 nuclear land-attack cruise missile (range: 3000 km).
[b] Anti-submarine missile carrying either a torpedo (SS-N-16) or a nuclear depth charge (SS-N-15), similar to US SUBROC.

The US Navy has 103 submarines for non-strategic roles, 98 of which are nuclear-powered. But, excluding 10 nuclear-powered submarines built before 1961 (the Skate and Skipjack Classes and two others) and 2 commando transport submarines converted from Ethan Allen Class SSBNs (bunks are installed in the former missile section), 86 nuclear-powered submarines are to be regarded as the US first-line attack submarine force compared with the Soviet Union's 50 SSGNs and 53 SSNs, which can be regarded as first-line nuclear-powered submarines with anti-ship/anti-submarine roles (excluding Echo II, Yankee conversion, Echo I, November, Hotel conversion). The US Navy has not built conventionally powered submarines since 1959, when 3 Barbel Class submarines were completed. In spite of their advantages of being quiet, less expensive than nuclear-powered ones and very effective for anti-submarine barrier patrols in choke points and for coastal defence, the US Navy does not want them because these missions can be allocated to US ally submarines.[13] (The USA's NATO allies have 143 submarines including 13 nuclear-powered and 116 conventionally powered attack submarines. In the Pacific, Japan has 14 and Australia has 6 submarines.) Being partly free from these defensive missions, US attack submarines can engage in such peacetime missions as: *(a)* tracking Soviet SSBNs and SSNs; *(b)* intelligence collection near the Soviet coast, especially near harbours; *(c)* guarding aircraft carrier battle groups and battleship surface action groups against Soviet SSGNs and SSNs; and *(d)* target service for ASW training. In wartime, their missions would include such operations as: *(a)* anti-submarine and anti-surface ship attack; *(b)* land attack with cruise missiles; *(c)* mining of Soviet harbours; and *(d)* also some barrier patrols (those not assigned to allied submarines).

For these purposes, the US Navy normally assigns four submarines to its 6th Fleet in the Mediterranean Sea, and six or more submarines to the 7th Fleet in the Western Pacific and Indian Oceans. The remaining attack submarines in its 2nd (Atlantic) and 3rd Fleets (Eastern Pacific, generally east of 160°E) perform some front-line missions in their respective areas (in addition to serving as training units). Included are: the Norwegian and Barents Seas approaching Soviet submarine bases on the coast of the Kola Peninsula; and in the Bering Sea to the east of Petropavlovsk on Kamchatka, where 24 of the Soviet SSBNs are based.

Reflecting asymmetrical US and Soviet strategic conditions and naval force structures, US attack submarines have been predominantly anti-submarine oriented, whereas Soviet submarines have been inclined towards the more traditional role of surface ship attacks, as the existence of special SSGs and SSGNs suggests. US submarines are armed with MK-48 wire-guided torpedoes basically designed for anti-submarine attacks. About 30 submarines (the first 12 of the Los Angeles Class, 11 of the Sturgeon Class and 7 of the Permit Class) are equipped with analogue MK-113 fire-control systems and can carry SUBROC (UUM-44A) torpedo-tube-launched anti-submarine missile carrying a nuclear depth charge (range: 56 km; 2-5 kt; W55 warhead). Each SUBROC-capable submarine is said to carry four to six missiles. Though the production of the SUBROC ended in 1978, since 1980 the US Navy has been developing its replacement 'ASW-SOW' (anti-submarine warfare stand-off weapon), to be named 'Sea Lance'. It is planned that 'Sea Lance' will be able to deliver either a homing torpedo or a nuclear-depth charge to a greater distance and will be compatible with the MK-117 digital fire-control system of newer submarines.

US SSNs have always had a great advantage over Soviet nuclear submarines in that they are much quieter. Early Soviet nuclear-powered submarines produced tremendous noises, from steam turbines, reduction gear, propellers and auxiliary machinery. Even Victor IIIs (21 built between 1978 and 1985), which are said to be much quieter than previous types and which constitute the mainstay of today's Soviet modern SSN force, can be noisier than the US Sturgeon Class built 10 years earlier. According to one estimate[14] they can be detected at a range of 20 to 500 nautical miles (37-900 km) in deep waters and 10 to 70 nautical miles (18-130 km) in shallow waters depending on underwater acoustic conditions. In contrast, the new US attack submarines of the Los Angeles Class (34 have been built since 1976) are as quiet as diesel-electric submarines operating on battery power, and they can be detected in the ranges of 1 to 25 nautical miles (1.8-46 km) in deep waters and 1 to 15 nautical miles (1.8-27 km) in shallow waters. The Ohio Class SSBNs are even quieter and cannot be detected until another submarine gets within 4 nautical miles (7.2 km) under the best acoustic conditions and within only 0.2 nautical miles (370 m) under the worst acoustic conditions.

Although the newest types of Soviet attack submarine, such as the Akula Class (two completed by 1987), must naturally be quieter than their predecessors, the USSR still seems to be much behind contemporary US submarines in quieting technology.

Numerically controlled lathes were exported to the Soviet Union by the Toshiba Machinery Co. between 1983 and 1984; they became operational in late 1984. This occurred after the Akula Class and other new quiet Soviet submarines were launched, with new type propellers, of course. US Undersecretary of Defense Richard Armitage wrote letters to members of the US Congress in 1988 to explain that the Soviet Union had developed quiet submarine propellers three years before they imported Japanese sophisticated processing machinery.

Moreover, the capabilities of submarine sonars are as important as quieting. There is, however, no open source material from which the exact capabilities of US sonars can be derived, this being one of the most sensitive pieces of information, to say nothing about information about the comparable Soviet sonars. But, judging from the efforts and experiences of the US Navy in the ASW area, long-term research in underwater acoustics and the relative level of the micro-electronics technology of the two countries, it would be rather safe to assume that the US Navy and its principal naval allies have considerable advantages in underwater detection systems. One of the clues to this is the fact that the Soviet Union's new anti-submarine frigates—Krivak Is and IIs (built 1970-84)—are known to have medium frequency sonars, while the US surface ships' SQS-23 sonars (operational in 1958) and the modernized SQS-53 or SQS-56 sonars are low frequency and have much longer detection ranges than the previous US medium-frequency sonars.

The other example that suggests the technological gap in underwater warfare is the huge size of SS-N-14 anti-submarine missiles of Soviet ships. The quadruple launcher of the SS-N-14, which first appeared in 1969 aboard the Kresta II cruiser, occupies about half of the Krivak's foredeck and has no reload missiles. Its US equivalent ASROC (*anti-submarine rocket*; operational in 1961), however, is much smaller and is usually carried in a compact octuple-box launcher; its small size enables many ships to carry reload missiles.

Most Soviet Navy ships still use standard 21-inch (533 mm in diameter) long torpedoes for anti-submarine roles, while the US Navy developed the 254-mm light-weight homing torpedo MK-43 in 1951 and later replaced this with the MK-44 and the MK-46 (324 mm) models. Today the USA is developing a fourth generation ASW torpedo called the MK-50. This seems to suggest that the Soviet electronics technology industry has been unable to produce small sonars effective enough to fit in light-weight torpedoes. A large sensor based on vacuum tube technology will mean a large torpedo. And when a large torpedo is used as the warhead of an anti-submarine missile, it will need a large booster rocket to fly. This will then mean a large launcher and finally a larger warship with small combat weapon loads. Although some Soviet coastal defence ships carry 406-mm torpedoes, new major surface ships are equipped with 533-mm tubes, and the newest Soviet submarines are equipped with staggeringly large (650-mm) torpedo tubes.

If Soviet technology requires a larger diameter than US technology to make a workable sonar for ASW torpedoes, then the bow-mounted sonars of Soviet submarines would not be as good as the sonars of US submarines because the sizes of the bow-mounted sonars cannot be so different. Another weak point about Soviet submarines is their heavy reliance on active sonars, perhaps reflecting the Soviet technological lag in underwater acoustics and computers necessary to make effective passive sonars. If a submarine uses an active sonar which emits powerful sound waves, the opponent equipped with a passive sonar can detect its presence long before it is itself detected. It is almost like a soldier in night battle who uses a flash light to find his enemy rather than a night vision device. In an underwater battle, a noisy submarine with an inferior sonar is vulnerable to a quiet submarine equipped with better sensors. The latter can destroy its opponent even before its existence is noticed.

While being primarily anti-submarine oriented, US submarines of course can attack surface ships. Their MK-48 torpedoes with 290-kg high-explosive warheads are effective against surface targets too. Most submarines can launch Harpoon (RGM-84) anti-ship missiles from torpedo tubes. The range of a Harpoon is 110 km with a 225-kg high-explosive warhead, and the range is being extended to 150 km.

The development of Tomahawk cruise missiles added another mission to US submarines—land attack. Although Tomahawks were first deployed in Western Europe as ground-launched cruise missiles (GLCMs) and are currently carried aboard US surface ships, originally they were developed for launching from the standard 533-mm torpedo tubes of submarines, as the missile's diameter suggests. The missile was designed based upon the concept that attack submarines would be able to perform supplementary strategic nuclear roles with nuclear-tipped cruise missiles. Its 2500-km range and 150-kt yield warhead (nuclear land-attack version; BGM-109A) gives it a strike capability almost equal to the early version of the Polaris A2 SLBM, which had a range of slightly less than 3000 km and had a single warhead. Though the Tomahawk 'family' includes an anti-ship version (BGM 109B) with a 450-kg conventional warhead (range: 450 km) and conventional land-attack versions (BGM-109C/D), the targeting problem for fully utilizing the long range of such anti-ship missiles, as with the Soviet Oscar Class submarines, are applicable to submarine-launched anti-ship Tomahawks. Also the effectiveness of conventional land-attack versions has to be deemed questionable because the terminal guidance required for conventional attacks has to be much more precise than for nuclear ones. The bomblets-dispenser warhead of BGM-109D, aimed at covering a wide area with numerous small bombs, can be effective against limited types of target, such as exposed aircraft. Therefore it is likely that Tomahawks carried aboard US attack submarines are mostly nuclear-armed land-attack versions, as originally conceived in Tomahawk development.

The fact that a US submarine can play various roles, whereas the Soviet Union has to build specialized types, contributed to the simplification of the composition of the US submarine fleet. While the Soviet Navy is building six types of submarine at the rate of 6.25 per year, including two types of strategic missile submarine, the US Navy is building one type of SSBN (Ohio Class) and a single type of SSN (Los Angeles Class).

The Los Angeles Class (6900 t; submerged; cost: $741-million per submarine) are now being built at the rate of four per year. This is a pace far exceeding that of Soviet nuclear-powered attack and anti-ship missile submarine (SSN/SSGN) construction, while the Western counterparts to the Soviet Navy's conventionally powered Kilo Class submarines are being built by many US allied navies.

From 1976 to 1986, 34 Los Angeles Class SSNs were commissioned. And by 1991, US Navy plans to have the funding of a total of 66 Los Angeles Class SSNs, thus making them the world's largest class of nuclear-powered submarines. This class is said to be about 5 knots faster than previous Sturgeon Class SSNs, whose speed was announced to be '30 knots plus'. So, obviously, they are much faster than the Soviet Union's Victor III with a reported 30-knot maximum speed. Though the Los Angeles Class submarines are not as fast as the Soviet Alfa Class (reported to be 42 knots), Alfas are thought to be even noisier than Soviet first generation nuclear-powered submarines. Perhaps Los Angeles Class submarines are at least as fast as any of the Soviet Union's new generation submarines to be deployed from the late

1980s, for example, Akula and Sierra, and are probably more quiet and advanced in sensor systems.

The fact that US submarines are more versatile and that the submarine inventory is simplified allows for greater simplicity in supply, maintenance and training. Normally, this would result in higher efficiency. However, the limited number of weapons that can be carried presents a problem. Usually a submarine such as the Los Angeles Class can carry about 25 torpedoes or other weapons. If it carries Tomahawk, Harpoon and acoustic decoys (to confuse other submarines or anti-submarine ships and aircraft), the number of MK-48 torpedoes has to be limited. Today, some carry SUBROCs, and in the future all will carry ASW-SOW anti-submarine missiles. Some submarines can lay mines, too. To solve this weapon-load mix problem, the later version of Los Angeles Class (33 submarines) will have 12 vertical launchers of Tomahawks between the inner pressure hull and the outer hull, thus permitting more space for other weapons.

Just before their (SSN-688) construction programme is completed, the US Navy wishes to proceed to the SSN-21 (or SEAWOLF) Class submarine programme (from fiscal year 1989). These submarines are designed to be bigger (10 000 t), faster and quieter than the Los Angeles Class submarines, and carry about 50 weapons, which is twice that of the Los Angeles Class. The US Navy aims at building about 30 SSN-21s. If this plan is implemented, the US Navy will be able to replace all of its older attack submarine fleet with the Los Angeles Class and the SSN-21 Class. Although at present it includes 41 SSNs that have to be retired by the year 2000, 17 of the Sturgeon Class commissioned after 1970 and one other (Lipscomb) will remain in active service during that year. If the first submarine of the SSN-21 Class can be commissioned in 1994 and their construction is continued at the pace of 2 per year from the 1991 budget onward, then the US Navy will have more than 90 SSNs by the year 2000. However, the Soviet submarine fleet in the year 2000 would have about 90 SSNs and SSGNs, instead of the present force of 120 or more assuming that the present speed of Soviet submarine construction remains the same.

Conclusion

In view of the technological differences between the USA and the Soviet Union, especially in computer-related fields, and because of the large submarine fleet of US allies, rough numerical parity between the

US and Soviet SSN forces would mean an overwhelming superiority for the West. Thus, even in the submarine field, as well as in the fields of aircraft carriers and surface ships, the West holds a significant advantage.

Nevertheless, the question remains whether the US Government's financial situation would allow the US Navy to continue to build extremely expensive submarines (the first of the SSN-21 Class is estimated to cost $1600 million) as well as many surface ships.

IV. Anti-submarine warfare capabilities

In order to assess accurately the degree of the Soviet submarine threat to the West, including US allies in the Pacific, quantitative and qualitative comparisons of submarine forces themselves are not sufficient because submarines are, although very effective, only one type of countermeasure to other submarines.

In ASW, various kinds of platform are mobilized, such as surface ships, patrol planes, helicopters and submarines. They carry numerous types of ASW sensor and weapon. In addition, acoustic and magnetic detection devices are layed on sea-beds.

As anti-tank weapons are one of the key factors in ground warfare, ASW capabilities are the most crucial element of naval warfare.

ASW technologies

One of the major research and development efforts of the US Navy and its allied navies since the 1960s has been in the area of anti-submarine warfare. As a result, the study of underwater acoustics has rapidly developed and has now become a branch of science regarding the propagation of sound in water, under complex conditions from various factors such as water temperature, depth, current and salinity, among others. This, coupled with the amazing advances in computer technologies in recent decades, has made it possible to block out background noises from other sources, such as sea currents and surface ships, in order to single out submarine acoustic signatures. These submarine acoustic signatures include sounds from steam turbines, reduction gears, propellers, pumps and other auxiliary machinery of nuclear-powered submarines. Although conventional diesel-electric-powered submarines produce less sound when operating underwater with an electric motor, they still make propeller and water friction noises from their hulls. In World War II and the post-war period, sonars of destroyers, frigates and other anti-submarine ships were basically active sonars which emitted sound waves into the water and then picked up the echoes reflected by a submarine's hull. But modern long-range acquisition sonars utilize passive technologies and listen to the underwater sounds with a huge array of hydrophones set beneath the hull, which pick up low-frequency sounds that reach further than high- or medium-frequency ones. Because of this, sonar ranges, which were only several thousand metres during World War II, are now measured by a scale of tens of kilometres. By comparing computer-processed submarine sound characteristics with pre-stored data, it has become possible to know the types and often even the individual identity of each submarine.

These advances in underwater acoustics were extensively utilized in the fixed submarine detection systems called SOSUS (Sound Surveillance System) which the US Navy has laid on the sea floors of the US East Coast since the early 1950s (the US Navy first acquired a cable layer for SOSUS in 1953). The US Navy has continued the improvement of the SOSUS and has expanded the deployment of it. Although details of SOSUS are not made public, its detection range is said to be hundreds of miles. SOSUS is believed to be arrays of hydrophones connected by long electric cables extending thousands of kilometres on ocean floors or the sea-bed.

Noises which hydrophones pick up are sent to shore terminals through cables to be processed and analysed by computers. It is believed that SOSUS arrays are installed in such areas of strategic importance as the US East and West Coasts, along the so-called 'GIUK gap' (a line between Greenland, Iceland and the UK), the Strait of Gibraltar and the North Western Pacific. It has been reported that their precision has been so improved that the US Navy is able to localize a submarine's position within a radius of some 90 km.[15]

If this assertion is right, it would amount to an area that can be covered by one P-3C anti-submarine aircraft. When the general position of a submarine is given to an ASW aircraft, it can search that area by dropping sonobuoys (a buoy containing a radio transmitter and a suspended hydrophone). Passive (listening) sonobuoys are sown in patterns to form sonobuoy barriers. They pick up underwater sounds and transmit them to ASW aircraft. One P-3C can carry up to 84 sonobuoys, can monitor the radio signals of 31 sonobuoys simultaneously and analyse the signals of 16 of them. By so doing, it can cover an area of 193 600 km^2, which is about 50 per cent larger than England.

Once a submarine noise is detected by passive sonobuoys, ASW aircraft can switch to active sonobuoys to determine exactly the submarine's position by echo-ranging (i.e., the process by which the echoes of sonar signals are used to locate submarines). Magnetic anomaly detectors (the long tail boom of ASW aircraft contains a coil for this purpose) are used to know more precise positions and to confirm that the underwater target has a steel hull, and that it is not a mistaken 'contact', such as a group of fish, a whale or a whirlpool. These are also the measures used to discriminate torpedo-type acoustic decoys, which are intended to produce acoustic signatures similar to those of a submarine.

Aboard the aircraft and at on-shore ASW operation centres, submarine acoustic signatures are processed and co-related with known signatures of various types to determine the submarine's identity. In a war situation, if the submarine is found to be a foe, ASW aircraft would drop an anti-submarine torpedo (MK-46 in the US Navy and most allied navies) that makes a spiral pattern search with its own active/passive sonar and homes in on the submarine. Because the Soviet Union's large submarines, such as Typhoon Class SSBNs, have a wide water-filled space between the inner pressure hull and the outer hull that can make the 43 kg high-explosive warhead of the US MK-46 torpedo less effective, a new MK-50 is now being developed that will have a shaped charge warhead, like those used in anti-tank missiles, so that its blast will be concentrated forward into the submarine's inner hull. Nuclear depth charges can also be carried by ASW aircraft and helicopters. The US Navy is believed to have some 897 B-57 ASW nuclear depth bombs (yield 5-20 kts).[16]

The utilization of an underwater acoustic phenomenon called the 'convergence zone (CZ)'—that is, underwater sound-waves will often come up to the surface every 50 to 60 kms in a concentric doughnut-like pattern—radically expanded the area that one ASW aircraft can search with its sonobuoys. In the past, sonobuoys and ships' sonars were only capable of picking up direct sound-waves. Today, in optimum conditions of a deep, stable sea, they can utilize the 'third CZ' and detect a submarine about 170 kms away.

As already mentioned, attack submarines are very effective ASW weapon systems, being able to listen to other submarine sounds in a stable and quiet deep sea. US submarines are equipped with huge bow-mounted sonars which occupy the entire bow section of submarines. The BQQ-5 sonar of the Los Angeles Class and some of the Sturgeon Class of the US Navy integrates bow sonars and towed array sonars (arrays of hydrophones towed by an 800-metre long cable) to achieve further long-range acquisition. This bow-mounted sonar, like many others, can be operated in an active mode also, to be used for echo ranging and in shallow waters where passive listening is often difficult.

For attacking enemy submarines, US submarines have MK-48 torpedoes which can be controlled from the launching submarine by electric signals sent through thin electric wire that comes out from the torpedo as it runs. The torpedo also has its own passive/active sonar, which guides it to the target at the terminal stage. Its range is reported to be 32 000 metres. Some 30 US submarines can carry 4 to 6 nuclear SUBROCs (UUM-44A), which are to be replaced by ASW-SOW (range: 110-170 kms; nuclear warhead or MK-50 homing torpedo). The development of the latter is to be completed by the year 1990.[17]

Mining has proved to be an effective countermeasure to submarines since the British Navy laid mine barriers in the North Sea in World War I. Today, the US Navy has the CAPTOR (en*cap*sulated *tor*pedo) mine (MK-60) which contains an MK-46 torpedo and sonar. It is laid in deep sea, and when its sonar detects a hostile submarine's signature, the torpedo will 'swim out' and hit the target. This revolutionary new mine can cover an area much wider than conventional mines that detonate either by contact or by influence caused by the passage of a ship or submarine such as a magnetic field or engine noise. CAPTORs facilitated the quick emplacement of mine-barriers by aircraft. Submarines can also launch SLIM (MK-67) torpedo-type self-propelled mines which penetrate into harbours or narrow channels and lie on the shallow sea bottom. When a SLIM senses the changes of the magnetic field or noises coming from a submarine or surface ship passing above, it explodes and causes damage to the target.

Aerial attacks against submarine bases were a very important part of anti-submarine operations in World War II. Allied bombers tried to destroy German submarines while in ports and damage shore support facilities. The Germans countered this by building thick concrete bunkers in submarine bases. Today, the US Navy's capability to attack Soviet naval bases comes from carrier-borne attack aircraft (A-6, A-7, F/A-18) and Tomahawk cruise missiles launched from surface ships and submarines. Air force bombers and tactical fighters (fighter bombers), too, can perform that role. The Soviet Navy is said to be building cave-type submarine bunkers in their submarine bases on the Kola Peninsula.[18]

Since World War II, there has been a continuous race between submarine development and ASW technologies. At the end of World War II, the British and US Navies managed to suppress German U-boats by building large numbers of escort ships and escort carriers converted from merchantmen (merchant ships). Also important for ASW have been sonars, surface-search radars, forward-throwing ASW mortars, and, above all, long-range patrol aircraft equipped with radars that could detect surfaced submarines or their snorkels (air intake and exhaust pipe extended above the surface for semi-submerged diesel operation).

The revolutionary development of submarines brought about by nuclear propulsion in the 1950s temporarily left ASW technology far behind. However, ASW technology has steadily developed since then. Today it seems that ASW has recovered some edge over submarines. This is especially true for the USA's and its close naval allies' ASW technology, *vis-à-vis* Soviet submarines. The fact that Soviet strategic missile submarines have to seek hiding places or 'bastions' in coastal waters, where US ASW aircraft and surface ships find it too risky to approach, or even under the Arctic ice, where sonobuoys and air-launched torpedoes are hard to use, seems to be proof of the present superiority of Western ASW technology over Soviet submarines.

All new Soviet submarines from the giant Typhoons to the conventionally powered Kilos are coated with anechoic tiles that absorb sound waves. The effectiveness of this coating in avoiding detection is, however, questionable since modern ASW is mostly based upon passive detections rather than active sonars, against which sound-absorbent coating can only be effective to a certain degree. It is possible that the Soviet Navy is aiming at confusing less powerful small active sonars of homing torpedoes by coating their submarines with such material.

Nevertheless, it has to be remembered that any technological edge is not permanent. It can be suddenly overthrown again if one technological breakthrough is achieved, such as the possible future development of noiseless propulsion. Also, the vulnerability of SOSUS—especially to air attacks in wartime, particularly shore terminals—would have to be taken into consideration.

Comparison of ASW forces

ASW forces of the USA and its allies

Because the large Soviet submarine fleet has been the most serious naval threat to the US Navy and its ally navies since the 1950s, and also due to the fact that submarines by nature have been a major threat to any surface ship, almost all surface combatants of the US Navy and its allies have sonars and ASW weapons (anti-air missile cruisers/ destroyers, too, have good ASW capability, and most US aircraft carriers carry 10 S-3A Viking ASW aircraft and 6 SH-6D ASW helicopters each). Four reactivated Iowa Class battleships lacking ASW capability are rare exceptions; however, they operate with large escort groups that have ASW capabilities. US and allied navies (including the French and Spanish Navies) have nearly 600 surface ships with ASW capability, about 800 fixed-wing ASW aircraft and more than 800 ASW helicopters (in some countries like the UK, ASW aircraft belong to the air forces).

The US Navy has 210 surface ships with ASW capability in active service and 515 fixed-wing ASW aircraft (including 13 reserve squadrons of P-3Bs), plus 264 ASW helicopters. Its 97 attack submarines (93 are nuclear-propelled) are mostly for the ASW role. With this, one should include 21 Coast Guard 'Cutters' that carry helicopters and have ASW capability.

Out of these, the US deploys 112 surface ships, 55 attack submarines and about half of its first-line ASW patrol aircraft forces (12 active P-3C squadrons) in the Atlantic and the Mediterranean. Other NATO countries, including France and Spain, have 281 surface ships, 157 fixed-wing ASW aircraft, 438 ASW helicopters and 133 attack submarines.

Therefore, the United States and its allies in the North Atlantic and Mediterranean have roughly 380 surface ships (excluding 10 Canadian ships in the Pacific), more than 180 submarines, about 400 fixed-wing ASW aircraft and about 550 ASW helicopters, against about 190 Soviet attack submarines (including anti-ship guided-missile submarines) and 39 ballistic missile submarines in the Soviet Northern Baltic and Black Sea fleets, plus 6 submarines from Bulgaria and Poland.

Although some part of the US, British and French attack submarine fleets would likely be used to protect their strategic missile submarines, and many smaller submarines of the NATO navies would be assigned for coastal defence against amphibious forces rather than for ASW purposes, many Soviet attack submarines will also have to play similar roles rather than disrupting Western shipping. (If we exclude the French and Spanish Navies, NATO's 11 navies in the Atlantic and Mediterranean will have roughly 310 surface ships, more than 160 submarines, 360 fixed-wing ASW aircraft and 500 ASW helicopters.)

In the Pacific, the US Navy has 100 surface ships with ASW capability, 42 attack submarines and another half of the ASW aircraft forces. Japan's Maritime Self-Defence Force has 52 ASW surface ships, 14 submarines, 118 fixed-wing ASW aircraft and 71 ASW helicopters. Australia, New Zealand, Canada (Pacific coast) and the Republic of South Korea in total have 39 surface ASW ships, 6 submarines, 44 fixed-wing ASW aircraft and 25 ASW helicopters (although 11 of 13 South Korean surface ships are of World War II design, and their main role is to cope with the North Korean Navy, which has 15 obsolete submarines, rather than the Soviet Pacific Fleet). In total, the United States and its allies in the Pacific have about 180 surface ships, 60 attack submarines, about 400 fixed-wing ASW aircraft and about 220 ASW helicopters against about 80 Soviet attack submarines (including anti-ship missile submarines) and 32 ballistic missile submarines in the Pacific. Large Western ASW patrol aircraft forces (400 each in the Atlantic/Mediterranean and in the Pacific) are particularly noteworthy because of the increasing roles and potential of ASW aircraft. Some of the factors that have increased the importance and potential of patrol aircraft forces in modern anti-submarine operations are: *(a)* their capabilities to survey a vast ocean space almost simultaneously with sonobuoys, radars and electronic signal-monitoring; *(b)* their quicker response to go to the scene of submarine attacks; *(c)* their better chances to utilize 'convergence zones'; *(d)* their improved all-weather capability; and *(e)* the rapid development of sonobuoys and signal-processing systems.

ASW forces of the USSR and its allies

The Soviet Navy, however, has also armed almost all of its surface combatants (about 270) with some ASW weapons. But it should be noted that less than 70 of them (Kiev, Moskva, Kirov, Kara, Kresta II, Udaloy and Krivak Classes) carry SSN-14 or other (SUW-N-1 aboard the Kiev and Moskva Classes) anti-submarine missiles, which are comparable to US ASROC (rocket-propelled ASW torpedo or nuclear depth charge) or Australian-developed Ikara and French Malafon ASW missiles, whereas more than 170 US and 42 Japanese, plus 51 ships of other US allies are equipped with ASROC or other ASW missiles.

Also some 30 Soviet Navy ships (Kiev, Kirov, Moskva, Kara, Kresta II, and Udaloy Classes) carry ASW helicopters (Ka-25 Hormone A or Ka-27 Helix A), and 12 others carry target acquisition helicopters for their anti-ship missiles. Compared with this, 171 US Navy ships (excluding many helicopter-carrying amphibious operation ships), 54 British, 22 Italian, 18 Dutch and 13 Japanese ships, plus 86 ships of other US allies (including France, Spain and Latin American nations) have helicopters whose primary purpose is ASW.

The 30 some Soviet ships carrying ASW helicopters are also equipped with ASW missiles, and about 30 more ships have missiles only. The remaining Soviet surface combatants (about 200) have only ASW torpedoes and multiple ASW rockets, which are somewhat similar to US Hedgehogs (multiple mortar) of World War II vintage, as their ASW weapons. Thus, it is doubtful whether these ships can effectively cope with nuclear-powered attack submarines and modern conventional submarines, which are quiet and fairly fast.

Having at least either one helicopter or anti-submarine missile system, or ideally both is regarded by Western navies as almost indispensable for a surface ship to conduct modern ASW operations. The reasons for this view are:

1. In order to utilize effectively the extended range of their sonars, some means of delivering a torpedo or depth charge to a distant target is required.

2. Nuclear submarines are often faster than surface ships and can easily get away from chasing surface ships that lack long-range and fast anti-submarine weapon delivery systems.

In the area of ASW aircraft, the Soviet Navy's inferiority is again obvious. It is believed to have 60 Tu-142 (Bear F), 50 Il-38 (May) and 100 Be-12 (Mail) compared with the US Navy's 515 fixed-wing ASW aircraft plus 300 of its allies. Furthermore, their quality has to be regarded as questionable. One hundred Mails are twin turbo-prop amphibious flying boats designed in the 1950s which are already obsolete. The present inventory of 100 Mails are what remain from some 200 aircraft produced. Bear Fs are four turbo-prop aircraft remodelled from long-range bomber aircraft, and Mays are remodelled from Il-18 passenger aircraft. Although it is believed that both Bear Fs and Mays are still being produced in small numbers, considering the Soviet computer technology in general, their sensors and processing systems are probably not up to the standard of the US P-3C.

However, trying to compare Soviet ASW capability with that of the United States and its allies may itself be illogical, because the Soviet Navy is almost completely lacking in sea-based airpower (aircraft carriers) and has little chance of establishing sea control, which is the prerequisite for open-sea ASW. (Germany in World Wars I and II did not need ASW forces.) For the Soviet Union, the meaning of ASW would be mainly the protection of its strategic missile submarines and naval and civilian ports from US submarines. But even in these limited coastal ASW missions the Soviet Union's performance would depend upon whether or not it could keep up with the pace of Western technological developments in submarine designs and highly advanced sensors, computers and underwater acoustics.

Conclusion

On balance, the USA and its allies have, and will continue to have, considerable advantages over the navies of the USSR and its allies. If the current trends in Western technology and in Soviet shipbuilding rates continue for the foreseeable future, the Western advantages will increase. However, fiscal restraints on the two major naval powers may compel them to scale back further their current naval plans. And, these restraints may be the only reliable form of naval arms control in the offing. The reason for this conclusion is that the great differences between the maritime dependence of both the East and the West along with the resultant naval forces of both sides have enormously complicated the attempts made at negotiating naval force limitations.

Notes and references

1   Whiting, K. R., *Soviet Air Power* (Westview Press: Boulder, CO, 1986), p. 186.
2   Cockburn, A., *The Threat* (Hutchinson & Co. Ltd: London, 1983), p. 251.
3   Whiting (note 1).
4   Sekai no Gun yo Ki, 'World's military aircraft', *Koku-Journal Tokyo* (1986), pp. 143ff.
5   Japan Air Self-Defence Force Public Relations Office issued press releases whenever its interceptors identified Backfires.

6 'Sea Lane Boei' (defence), *Asahi Shimbun* Booklet No. 31, p. 54.

7 *United Nations Statistical Yearbook 1983/84*, pp. 1025-40.

8 *United Nations* (note 7).

9 *Jane's Fighting Ships 1986-87*, p. 533.

10 See, e.g., Wilson, G. C., 'Submarine sinks as Russians try to tow it to port', *International Herald Tribune*, 7 Oct. 1986; and US Information Service *Wireless File*, 'Liquid fuel propellant probable cause of Soviet sub mishap', 6 Oct. 1986, US Embassy, Stockholm, Sweden.

11 *Jane's Weapon Systems 1986-87*, p. 6. The SS-13s CEP is estimated to be 1800 m.

12 Polmar, N., *The Ships and Aircraft of the US Fleet*, 13th edn (Naval Institute Press: Annapolis, MD, 1984), p. 44.

13 *Building a 600-Ship Navy: Costs, Timing and Alternative Approaches*, Congressional Budget Office, p. 68.

14 Stefanik, T. A., 'America's maritime strategy—the arms control implications', *Arms Control Today*, vol. 16, no. 9 (Dec. 1986), see graph on p. 12.

15 See Daniel, D. C., *Anti-submarine Warfare and Superpower Strategic Stability*, IISS (Macmillan: London, 1986), p. 124; and Tsipis, K., 'Antisubmarine warfare—fact and fiction', *New Scientist*, 16 Jan. 1975, pp. 145-7.

16 *SIPRI Yearbook 1987, World Armaments and Disarmament* (Oxford University Press: Oxford, 1987), p. 7.

17 Polmar (note 12), p. 436.

18 *Soviet Military Power 1987* and *Soviet Military Power 1986*, US Department of Defense (US Government Printing Office: Washington, DC), p. 28 and pp. 20-1, respectively.

Part II. The naval nuclear arms race

Chapter 3. Naval nuclear weapons: status and implications

Richard Fieldhouse

I. Introduction

Nuclear weapons are the most important but most overlooked aspect of naval forces. Between one-quarter and one-third of all the nuclear weapons in the world are assigned to naval forces. Yet, aside from ballistic missiles carried by the submarines of five nations, naval nuclear weapons have received little attention, whether in professional naval circles, at arms control negotiations or in the public domain. Nuclear weapons are central to the navies of the USA, the USSR, the UK, France and China. All of these nations, except China, place a significant portion of their strategic nuclear warheads on submarine-launched ballistic missiles (SLBMs), and all but China also possess what are loosely called 'tactical' nuclear weapons, that is, basically anything other than the 'strategic' SLBMs. These navies routinely carry nuclear weapons aboard their naval vessels, and any conflict emerging between nuclearized navies would hold the inherent risk of escalating to a nuclear war.

In the context of arms control, it is remarkable that tactical or non-strategic naval nuclear weapons have been ignored for more than 30 years. This is particularly so if one considers that these weapons are similar in function to other nuclear weapons that have long been the focus of arms control and security concerns. For example, the Soviet SS-20 missiles and the US Pershing II and ground-launched cruise missiles (GLCMs) based in Europe (often called intermediate-range nuclear forces, or INF) have been the subject of great concern, and the superpowers have negotiated an agreement to eliminate them globally. Meanwhile, sea-launched cruise missiles (SLCMs) that are expected to be more numerous and under fewer political constraints than their land-based counterparts have received far less attention, although they have similar destructive capabilities.

Tactical naval nuclear weapons, however, are different from other nuclear weapons in several respects that have permitted them to escape the attention of arms control efforts, as well as other forms of public scrutiny. Naval nuclear weapons have traditionally been of less concern to the public because it is presumed that naval warfare—and any consequent nuclear explosions—would take place at sea, far from population centres. Out of sight, out of mind. Being based at sea, naval nuclear weapons do not bring about the visibility or the controversies of basing on land (foreign or domestic). Their presence is not felt except perhaps by residents of naval ports or harbours where nuclear-capable ships call. A decision to use them would be made on a unilateral basis and not by a group of allied nations. Perhaps most importantly, there has been negligible public discussion by navy or government officials of tactical naval nuclear weapons compared to the voluminous literature on other types of nuclear weapon.[1] Thus the public has remained largely uninformed on issues concerning such forces. There has, however, been growing international interest in the 1980s in the naval arms race and in the nuclear weapons of the nuclear navies, particularly of the superpowers.[2]

This chapter examines the types and numbers of nuclear weapon deployed with and planned for the five nuclear navies, along with their implications for arms control and armed conflict. It begins with a discussion of the role of nuclear weapons in naval forces and in the larger context of general nuclear forces. Section II of this chapter explains the different categories of naval nuclear weapons—strategic and non-strategic—for each of the relevant nations, and is followed, in sections III and IV, respectively, by a detailed presentation of those forces. The chapter concludes in section V with an assessment of the implications of these nuclear weapons for arms control and armed conflict.

II. Nuclear weapons and naval forces

Naval nuclear weapons are important to the five acknowledged nuclear weapon nations: the USA, the USSR, the UK, France and China. Each of these nations places a considerable portion of its strategic nuclear warheads on SLBMs; they are considered the least vulnerable element of its nuclear arsenal. For the USA, SLBMs comprise 43 per cent of its entire strategic arsenal; the USSR places some 31 per cent of its strategic warheads on SLBMs; and for the UK, France and China, estimates are 34, 87 and 11 per cent, respectively (see table 12). In addition to these 9700 strategic weapons, nearly 6600 non-strategic weapons are deployed with the navies of the USA, the USSR, the UK and France, almost 16 300 nuclear weapons in all. The only arms control restraints specifically limiting naval nuclear weapons are those contained in the Strategic Arms Limitation Talks (SALT I and II) agreements between the USA and the USSR, which put limits on the number of 'modern' ballistic missile submarines permitted, and on the number of missile launchers they may carry. With the recent exception of SLCMs, no other naval nuclear weapons have even been considered in arms control negotiations, let alone subject to limitation.

In order to assess the impact of naval nuclear weapons, it is important to consider the type, function and number of these weapons, and their implications for the naval arms race, for arms control and for the likelihood or consequences of armed conflict. There has been remarkably little thought given to these subjects over the last 40 years, even though naval nuclear forces have been an important part of the nuclear arms race.

Nuclear weapons have fundamentally changed the nature of warfare, no less so for naval forces than for others, although this fact is often forgotten. For naval forces this fact has been manifested by two important changes: the deployment of nuclear weapons with navies (the creation of nuclear navies) and the consequences of nuclear weapons for naval warfare (rendering traditional naval forces and roles irrelevant in a nuclear war).

Two general types of nuclear weapon have been integrated into naval forces. The first is the strategic submarine with ballistic missiles. Such forces have advantages of mobility and stealth over fixed, land-based systems, and are therefore considered less vulnerable to attack than their land-based counterparts. Strategic (ballistic missile-equipped) submarines, either nuclear-powered (SSBNs) or conventionally powered (SSBs), perform their duties by staying hidden while keeping within range of their missiles' targets.

'Tactical' (or non-strategic) weapons are the second type of naval nuclear weapon, although many such weapons can serve similar purposes to the SLBMs—attacking land targets on foreign territory. The distinction between such land-attack weapons and strategic SLBMs is becoming more blurred with the introduction of modern long-range nuclear SLCMs into both the US and Soviet Navies. So-called tactical or non-strategic naval nuclear weapons can usefully be divided into two

Table 12. SLBM warheads as a percentage of strategic arsenals—1988

	Land-based missile	SLBM	Bomber	Total strategic warheads	SLBM % of total
USSR	6846	3670	1170	11686	31
USA	2300	5632	5070	13002	43
UK	0	128	245	373	34
France	18	256	18	292	87
China	145	24	50	219	11

Sources: The following sources were used to prepare the tables in part II, chapter 3 (tables 12—32). Handler, J. and Arkin, W. M., *Nuclear Warships and Naval Nuclear Weapons: A Complete Inventory*, Neptune Papers No. 2 (Greenpeace and Institute for Policy Studies: Washington, DC, May 1988); *SIPRI Yearbook 1988: World Armaments and Disarmament*, Stockholm International Peace Research Institute (Oxford University Press: Oxford, 1988); Cochran, T. B., Arkin, W. M. and Norris, R. S., *The Bomb Book: The Nuclear Arms Race in Facts and Figures* (Natural Resources Defense Council: Washington, DC, 1987); Arkin, W. M., *The Nuclear Arms Race at Sea*, Neptune Papers No. 1 (Greenpeace and Institute for Policy Studies: Washington, DC, 1987); US Joint Chiefs of Staff, *Military Posture FY 1989* (US Government Printing Office: Washington, DC, 1988); US Department of Defense, Secretary of Defense, *Annual Report to the Congress FY1989* (US Government Printing Office: Washington, DC, 1988); US Department of Defense, *Soviet Military Power*, 1st, 2nd, 3rd, 4th, 5th, 6th and 7th editions (US Government Printing Office: Washington, DC, annual); Polmar, N., *Guide to the Soviet Navy*, 4th edition (Arms and Armour Press: London, 1986); Moore, J. Captain, Royal Navy (ed.), *Jane's Fighting Ships 1986-87* (Jane's: London, 1986); Cochran, T. B., Arkin, W. M. and Hoenig, M. M., *Nuclear Weapons Databook, Volume 1: US Nuclear Forces and Capabilities* (Ballinger: Cambridge, MA, 1984); US Navy, Office of the Chief of Naval Operations, *Understanding Soviet Naval Developments*, 5th edition (NAVSO P-3560, Rev. 4/85) (US Government Printing Office: Washington, DC, 1985); US Department of Defense, Defense Intelligence Agency, *Unclassified Communist Naval Orders of Battle*, DDB-1200-124-86 (Defense Intelligence Agency: Washington, DC, Apr. 1986); author's estimates.

categories: those for attacks against land targets and those for warfare *at sea*.

Strategic submarines and SLBMs have traditionally been considered separately from the non-strategic weapons. SLBMs are widely credited (on the basis of supposition) with serving a 'stabilizing' role in the nuclear arms race, although current developments might challenge this assumption.[3] And since they undeniably belong to the superpowers' strategic nuclear forces, they have been included in US-Soviet arms control agreements and negotiations, including the 1972 SALT I agreement and the 1979 SALT II Treaty, and in the Strategic Arms Reductions Talks (START) being conducted in Geneva under the umbrella of the Nuclear and Space Talks (NST).

Tactical naval nuclear weapons have seldom been discussed in any arms control fora and, with the recent exception of SLCMs, have not been included in any bilateral or multilateral arms control negotiations. (Despite their many strategic characteristics, nuclear land-attack SLCMs have not been considered strategic weapons, in large part to exclude them from arms control. At their Washington summit meeting of 7-10 December 1987, the USA and the USSR agreed to find a way to limit long-range nuclear-armed SLCMs—the one category of weapons excluded from the START negotiations.) Basically, until the 1980s the existence of non-strategic nuclear weapons was not commonly known outside of naval and defence circles, although even within those groups they have been given surprisingly little serious thought.[4]

The development of naval strategic nuclear capabilities has taken navies away from their traditional roles and put them in the position of being able to inflict unprecedented destruction to other nations, ostensibly in order to dissuade those nations from attacking. Today's ballistic missile submarines (SSBs and SSBNs) operate almost as separate branches of their respective navies; they are components of long-range missile forces that the navies happen to operate only because navies own the ships and submarines. For the five nuclear navies this is an added dimension of their responsibilities that no other navies have. Strategic submarines and SLBMs are also the only types of nuclear weapon common to all five nuclear weapon nations—their essential symbol of superpower status.

The second major change brought to naval forces by nuclear weapons is that they have changed the very basis of naval power. Such weapons would, if used, render the traditional role of naval forces irrelevant. It is implausible that naval forces will be able to fight conventional battles of World War II style after the initial use of nuclear weapons in any US-Soviet war. This is because naval forces will become both high priority nuclear targets in a war and themselves the means of waging nuclear war. (A submarine that has the potential to destroy more than 150 targets—cities—takes on a different character than a vessel built to enforce a naval blockade. It is also a vastly more important target.)

Ships and aircraft are particularly susceptible to the effects of nuclear explosions, especially since they have no protection from their surrounding environment, while submarines are susceptible to underwater effects. No ship could withstand a nuclear blast of relatively low yield (1-10 kt) at a close distance. Given the destructiveness of nuclear weapons, their warheads can detonate quite far from a target and still cause critical damage to it, while non-nuclear weapons must strike the target or come within a few metres to have even a crippling effect. This is one of the reasons that nuclear weapons could be considered useful and usable in a war: they need not be as accurate as conventional weapons but they assure a high probability of destroying the target. In justifying US tactical naval nuclear weapons, Secretary of Defense Caspar Weinberger referred euphemistically to these factors as 'unique capabilities that serve as a backup for our conventional systems'.[5] Naval forces have become integral components of nuclear forces (and vice versa) and cannot be thought of as otherwise.

Consequently, a snapshot of the nuclear forces of the five nuclear navies (as of June 1988) is as follows. The Soviet Navy is the most highly nuclearized navy in the world, although the USA has a far larger number of naval nuclear warheads (9277 US compared to 6391 Soviet; see table 13). Concerning Soviet non-strategic naval capabilities, the US Joint Chiefs of Staff report that, 'almost all major surface combatants (about 290), all submarines (about 340) as well as a few of the other combatant ships (some 31) carry at least one if not a mix of systems'.[6]

Including its strategic submarine forces, Soviet naval nuclear-capable forces have: 77 ballistic missile submarines, 63 cruise missile submarines, 199 attack submarines, 6 V/STOL (vertical/short take-off and landing) aircraft carriers, 39 cruisers, 69 destroyers, 118 frigates and 56 patrol craft. In addition, Soviet naval aircraft include 370 attack aircraft and 390 anti-submarine warfare (ASW) aircraft capable of using nuclear weapons. Thus, the Soviet nuclear navy is comprised of some 627 ships and submarines and 760 aircraft (see table 14).

The nuclear-capable ships and submarines of the US Navy include: 36 ballistic missile submarines, 89 attack submarines, all 14 active aircraft carriers, 5 V/STOL aircraft carriers, 3 battleships, all 36 cruisers, all 64 destroyers and 65 frigates; 312 vessels in all. The US Navy also operates land- and sea-based nuclear-capable aircraft. For use aboard surface ships there are 1129 aircraft, 187 fixed-wing ASW aircraft and 128 ASW helicopters; there are 347 active land-based ASW aircraft or 1791 nuclear-capable aircraft in all (see table 15).

Britain's nuclear navy consists of 4 ballistic missile submarines, 3 aircraft carriers, 12 destroyers and 8 frigates. The Royal Navy operates nuclear-capable aircraft from ships (34 attack aircraft and 134 ASW helicopters). France has 6 ballistic missile submarines and 2 aircraft carriers. Nuclear-capable naval aviation consists of 36 attack aircraft for the carriers and 31 on land. China has three ballistic missile submarines, one of which has been officially declared operational. It is possible that some of China's stockpile of nuclear bombs may be available for its naval bomber force. It is estimated that these three smaller naval nuclear powers have some 578 naval nuclear warheads among them (see table 16) although this number will grow considerably in the 1990s.

Table 13. Naval nuclear weapons—1988

	USA	USSR	UK	France	China	Total
Strategic warheads	5632	3670	128	256	24	*9710*
Non-strategic warheads	3645	2721	168	36	0	*6570*
Total	*9277*	*6391*	*296*	*292*	*24*	*16280*

Sources : See table 12.

Table 14. Soviet nuclear-capable naval forces—1988

Type	Number	Class or model
Submarines		
Ballistic missile	77	Typhoon, Delta IV/III//II/I, Yankee II/I, Hotel III, Golf V/III/II
Cruise missile	63	Oscar, Papa, Charlie II/I, Echo II, Juliett, Yankee
Attack	<u>199</u>	Akula, Alfa, Mike, Sierra, Yankee, Victor III/II/I, Echo I, Hotel II, November, Kilo, Tango, Foxtrot, Romeo, Whiskey, Zulu
	339	
Surface ships		
Aircraft carriers[a]	6	Kiev, Moskva
Cruisers	39	Kirov, Kara, Kresta I/II, Kynda, Slava, Sverdlov
Destroyers	69	Sovremennyy, Udaloy, Kashin, Mod. Kashin, Conv. Kashin, Kildin, Mod. Kildin, Kanin, SAM Kotlin, Skoryy
Frigates	118	Krivak I/II, Riga, Grisha I/III/IV/V
Patrol combatants	<u>56</u>	Nanuchka I/III, Tarantul III, Turya, Sarancha
	288	
Aircraft		
Strike/bombers	370	Backfire B/C, Badger C/G, Blinder
ASW	<u>390</u>	Bear F, Mail, May, Hormone A, Helix A
	760	

[a] These ships carry helicopters and V/STOL aircraft only.

Sources: See table 12.

Table 15. US nuclear-capable naval forces—1988

Type	Number	Class or model
Submarines		
Ballistic missile	36	Ohio, Franklin, Madison Lafayette
Attack	89 / 125	Los Angeles, Sturgeon, Permit, Narwhal, Lipscomb
Surface ships		
Aircraft carriers[a]	19	Nimitz, Enterprise, Kennedy Kitty Hawk, Forrestal, Midway, (Tarawa)
Battleships	3	Iowa
Cruisers	36	Ticonderoga, Virginia, California, Truxtun, Bainbridge, Long Beach, Belknap, Leahy
Destroyers	64	Spruance, Adams, Farragut
Frigates	65 / 187	Brooke, Glover, Knox, Garcia, Bronstein
Aircraft		
Attack aircraft	1129	A-6E, A-7E, F/A-18, A-4M, AV-8B
ASW aircraft	662 / 1791	P-3B/C, S-3A/B, SH-3D/H

[a] This includes five Tarawa Class amphibious assault ships with nuclear-capable V/STOL aircraft.

Sources : See table 12.

Table 16. British, French and Chinese nuclear-capable naval forces—1988

Type	Number	Class or model	Warheads deployed
U K			
Ballistic missile submarines	4	Resolution	128
Surface ships			
Aircraft carriers	3	Invincible	
Destroyers	12	Type 42	
Frigates	8	Type 22	
Aircraft			
Carrier aircraft[a]	34	Sea Harrier FRS.1	34
ASW helicopters[b]	134	Sea King HAS.5, Lynx HAS.2/3	134
			262
France			
Ballistic missile submarines	6	Redoutable, Inflexible	256
Surface ships			
Aircraft carriers	2	Clemenceau	
Carrier aircraft	36	Super Etendard	36
			292
China			
Ballistic missile submarines	3	Xia, Golf	24
Bombers[c]	c	B-6 Badger, B-5 Beagle	c
Total naval nuclear weapons (UK, France and China)			*578*

[a] These aircraft operate from the three aircraft carriers.

[b] These helicopters operate from all three classes of nuclear-capable surface ship.

[c] Some 150 land-based bombers assigned to naval aviation are nuclear-capable. It is possible that nuclear bombs stockpiled for the air force would be available for these naval bombers, but they are not *naval* nuclear weapons.

Sources: See table 12.

It is essential to emphasize that accurate assessments of Soviet naval nuclear weapons are exceedingly difficult for one reason: the USSR makes absolutely no information available about such forces. Consequently, all the facts and analyses of Soviet naval nuclear forces—particularly estimates of the composition and size of its arsenal—are based on information from Western sources, primarily the USA. There are many gaps in this information and many unproven assumptions underlie it. Hence, there is a considerable degree of uncertainty about many of the details concerning Soviet naval nuclear weapons and practices. Although the basic trends and information appear reasonably reliable, the USSR should realize that its excessive secrecy is counter-productive. It makes Western observers more suspicious and fearful of the Soviet Navy than is warranted. It also makes attempts at co-operation regarding security and arms control vastly more difficult than they are inherently.

III. Strategic naval nuclear forces

Every day the five nuclear weapon nations operate an average combined total of 47 SSBNs at sea (25 US, 15 Soviet, 2 British, 3 French and 2 Chinese) carrying more than 5100 warheads. Of these, an average of 34 strategic submarines carrying more than 4000 warheads are on patrol and ready to fire (20 US, 10 Soviet, 1 British, 2 French and 1 Chinese). Each warhead is presumed to be assigned to a target on an adversary's homeland. Strategic submarines, particularly those of the USA and the USSR, are suitable to serve as nuclear 'reserve' forces that would be held back during a war so that there would still be nuclear forces available after the initial attacks had ended. However, strategic submarine/missile forces are undergoing improvements in accuracy to such a degree that they will be able to strike targets that have previously been assumed vulnerable only to land-based intercontinental ballistic missile (ICBM) attacks. These changes will bring new dangers and reactions to the nuclear arms race.

Strategic submarine operations typically follow a general pattern, although the specific practices of each country vary considerably. Each of the five nations operates a fleet of submarines larger than the number of submarines it operates at sea, but the ratio of submarines at sea to those in port differs widely. Submarines go to sea for periods (called patrols) of up to 70 days; part of each patrol is spent in transit between the homeport and the operating location where submarines are 'on station'. In order to remain undetected most submarines operate as quietly and unobtrusively as possible. This requires that they travel slowly (in order to minimize noise) and receive only one-way communications from their headquarters (in order to avoid giving away one's location by transmitting signals that can be intercepted). As with other strategic nuclear weapons, SSBNs require special communications to assure that they remain under the control of central political authorities. In the case of US submarines, messages are sent via various systems and frequencies to submerged submarines on a continuous basis to maintain such 'connectivity'.

Of the submarines at sea, some are on station; some are in transit; and others are in training or on sea trials. Of the submarines in port some are being refurbished for the next patrol; usually some are undergoing maintenance or repair; and others can be used for dockside training. In order to maximize the capability of a nuclear-powered submarine, some countries assign two crews to each submarine, so that each submarine spends as much time on patrol and as little time in port as possible.

Soviet strategic submarines

The USSR maintains the largest fleet of ballistic missile submarines in the world. It comprises 77 submarines, including 62 'modern' SSBNs (as defined in the SALT I agreement), 12 older SSBs and 3 test and training vessels (see table 17). These submarines carry 978 SLBMs and as many as 3670 warheads for theatre and intercontinental missions. Ballistic missile submarines apparently are still accorded lower priority than the land-based missiles of the Soviet Strategic Rocket Forces, but are being modernized at a steady pace. SSBN operational rates are much lower than the other nuclear navies: typically some 15-20 per cent of the fleet (10-12 submarines) are at sea, of which perhaps 60 per cent (7-10 submarines) are on station.[7] It is possible that the USSR keeps another 15-20 per cent of its SSBNs ready in port to fire missiles, but also ready to go to sea on short notice.[8]

The Soviet strategic submarine force consists of 11 different classes of submarine and 7 different types of SLBM (see table 18). While these numbers may appear impressive, it should be noted that the results are somewhat less so. Four classes of submarine consist of only one submarine each (Hotel III, Golf III, Yankee II and Golf V).

Table 17. Soviet strategic submarine forces—1988

Number and class	First year deployed	Number and type of missile	Warheads per missile	Total warheads deployed
5 Typhoon[a]	1983	20 x SS-N-20	10 MIRV	1000
4 Delta IV[b]	1986	16 x SS-N-23	4 MIRV	256
14 Delta III	1977	16 x SS-N-18	7 MIRV	1568
4 Delta II	1976	16 x SS-N-8	1	64
18 Delta I	1973	12 x SS-N-8	1	216
1 Yankee II	1977	12 x SS-N-17	1	12
16 Yankee I[c]	1967	16 x SS-N-6	2 MRV	512
12 Golf II[d]	1965	3 x SS-N-5	1	36
1 Golf III[e]	1973	6 x SS-N-8	1	6
1 Golf V[f]	1980	1 x SS-N-20	0	0
1 Hotel III[g]	1965	6 x SS-N-8	1	0
Total				*3670*

[a] 5 launched, 4 operational.

[b] 4 launched, 2 operational.

[c] Only Yankee I and above are counted as 'modern' submarines in SALT I.

[d] These are considered 'theatre' systems, which are being phased out.

[e] Test submarine for SS-N-8 missile; considered operational and armed.

[f] Test submarine for SS-N-20 missile; not considered armed.

[g] Test submarine for SS-N-8 missile; not considered armed.

Sources: See table 12.

The Golf V Class is a research and test vessel used in the Black Sea. Another class (Golf II) is obsolescent, is approaching the end of its service life and is armed with three old single-warhead missiles (SS-N-5) that have a range of 1400 km. The 12 submarines of this class are used in theatre roles in the Baltic Sea and in the Sea of Japan,[9] but may not be kept in service much longer as they are of limited value.

Of the seven types of SLBM, one is the SS-N-5 aboard the Golf II Class submarines, one is the 12 SS-N-17 missiles aboard the one Yankee II Class submarine, and one is the SS-N-6 which has two multiple re-entry vehicle (MRV) warheads that can strike only one target and which has a range of up to 3000 km. It was an exploding SS-N-6 missile that caused a Soviet Yankee I Class submarine to sink in October 1986 in the Atlantic Ocean. Of these seven missile types, only one successfully uses solid fuel (the SS-N-20); the solid-fuel SS-N-17 has been deployed on only one submarine and has insufficient range to operate in protected Soviet waters. Moreover, the most recent Soviet SLBM (the SS-N-23) uses liquid fuel, indicating continuing problems with solid fuel technology.

Table 18. Soviet SLBMs—1988

Type	Number deployed	First year deployed	Range (km)	Warheads x yield	Warheads deployed	Submarines
SS-N-5	36	1963	1400	1 x 1 Mt	36	On Golf II Class 'theatre' systems
SS-N-6	256	1973	3000	2 x 0.375-1 Mt (MRV)[a]	512	Yankee I
SS-N-8	286	1973	7800	1 x 1 - 1.5 Mt	286	Delta II/I, Golf III, Hotel III
SS-N-17	12	1977	3900	1 x .0.5-1 Mt	12	Yankee II
SS-N-18[b]	224	1978	6500/ 8000	7 x 200-500 kt	1568	Delta III
SS-N-20	100[c]	1983	8300	10 x 100 kt	1000	Typhoon
SS-N-23	64	1986	7240	4 x 100 kt	256	Delta IV
Totals	*978*				*3670*	

[a] SS-N-6 is sometimes counted as having 1 warhead, as at START, although 2 MRV warheads are carried.

[b] One modification of the SS-N-18 carries a single warhead and has the longer range.

[c] The US counts missiles deployed on submarines even before they are considered fully operational, thus 100 SS-N-20s and 64 SS-N-23s.

Sources: See table 12.

The Soviet Navy has been modernizing its SSBN/SLBM force steadily during the 1980s. The most important additions have been the deployments of two new classes of submarine: the Typhoon and the Delta IV, with their two new SLBMs—the SS-N-20 and the SS-N-23, respectively. These systems add to the growing proportion of submarines and missiles that are capable of striking targets in the USA from Soviet home waters, thus reducing the need to expose the submarine force to adversary ASW forces. Modern Soviet submarines are reported by US defence officials to operate in the Arctic Ocean under the ice for self-protection (this possibility is used as a justification for building US attack submarines that can find and destroy Soviet SSBNs under the ice). The two newest models of SLBM also are increasing the proportion of SLBMs that are equipped with multiple independently targetable re-entry vehicles (MIRVs), now at 23 submarines with 388 missiles, as it was only in 1977 that MIRVing of SLBMs began with the SS-N-18 missile.[10]

Soviet SSBNs are assigned mostly to one of two fleets—either the Northern Fleet (the largest submarine fleet), or the Pacific Fleet. The Northern Fleet has 38 submarines of the following Classes: 24 Delta, 9 Yankee and all 5 Typhoon SSBNs; while the Pacific Fleet has 16 Delta and 8 Yankee Class submarines of different models.[11] There are four primary base areas for SSBNs: Polyarnyy and Iokanga on the Kola Peninsula for the Northern Fleet and Vladivostok or Petropavlovsk for the Pacific Fleet.

US strategic submarines

The United States places more strategic nuclear weapons on its SLBMs than any other nation. The current force of 36 SSBNs is equipped with over 5600 warheads on 640 SLBMs, because of extensive MIRVing. The SSBN force basically consists of two types of submarine (i.e., Poseidon and Trident) and two types of missile that yield three different combinations: 16 Poseidon (including Lafayette, Franklin and Madison Classes) SSBNs, carrying 16 Poseidon C3 SLBMs each; 12 former Poseidon (Franklin and Madison Classes) SSBNs, carrying 16 Trident C4 SLBMs each; and 8 Trident (Ohio Class) SSBNs, each carrying 24 Trident C4 missiles (see table 19). Given this complexity of classes, these submarines are frequently referred to by the missiles they carry, hence Poseidon or Trident *submarines*. The 12 former Poseidon submarines that are fitted with Trident missiles were converted beginning in 1979 to carry the newer missiles.

A new missile, the Trident II or D5, is being developed and will be deployed beginning with the ninth Ohio Class submarine shortly after the first squadron of eight has finished receiving its full complement of

Table 19.   US strategic submarine forces - 1988

Type, number and class	First year deployed	Number and type of missile	Warheads per missile	Launchers deployed	Warheads deployed
Trident					
8 Ohio	1982	24 x Trident I C4	8	192	1536
6 Franklin/ 6 Madison	1979[a]	16 x Trident I C4	8	192	1536
Poseidon					
8 Lafayette/ 2 Madison/ 6 Franklin	1971[b]	16 x Poseidon C3	10	256	2560
Totals					
36				*640*	*5632*

[a] These 12 submarines were converted to carry Trident I C4 missiles beginning in 1979, although they were first operational in the mid-1960s with Polaris A3 missiles and (later) with Poseidon C3 missiles.

[b] These 16 submarines were converted to carry Poseidon C3 missiles beginning in 1969, from Polaris A3.

Sources: See table 12.

C4 missiles in 1989. D5 missiles will also be placed ('backfitted') aboard the first eight Ohio Class submarines, replacing their current Trident I (C4) missiles. The D5 missile will be the most accurate SLBM in any arsenal when it is deployed and, according to the Joint Chiefs of Staff (JCS), will be accurate enough to destroy hardened targets.[12] This heralds the transformation of SSBN/SLBM forces from weapons considered primarily as an invulnerable second-strike force to those capable of being used to try to destroy an adversary's nuclear forces in a pre-emptive attack. This 'counterforce' capability will change the perceived role of SSBNs fundamentally, and will likely bring a renewed emphasis on anti-submarine warfare to the arms race.

US SSBNs have been carrying MIRVed SLBMs since 1971 with the introduction of the Poseidon C3 missiles, thus accounting for the high warhead-to-missile ratio (see table 20). Each successive missile type has also had a greater range potential than the preceding model, permitting a greater area in which the submarines can patrol within range of their targets. Trident submarines equipped with the C4 SLBM can patrol in operating areas 16 times larger than those available to Poseidon submarines, thus affording improved security for the SSBN force. Although the D5 missile is potentially able to fly 2000 nautical miles further than the C4, the navy is using its additional throw weight for heavier warhead capacity.

Table 20. US SLBMs—1988

Type	Number deployed	First year deployed	Range (km)	Warheads x yield	Warheads deployed
Poseidon C3	256	1971	4600	10 x 40 kt	2560
Trident I C4	384	1979	7400	8 x 100 kt	3072
Trident II D5	0	1989	7500	8 x 475 kt	0
Totals	*640*				*5632*

Sources: See table 12.

Although Poseidon C3 missiles could theoretically carry as few as 6 and as many as 14 warheads, the number actually deployed is 10, for a total of 160 warheads in each Poseidon SSBN. Each warhead has a yield of 50 kt. The C3 missiles and the Lafayette, Franklin and Madison Class SSBNs carrying them are scheduled to remain in service until 1994, when they are expected to begin retirement. If past arms control provisions (SALT I and SALT II) are observed, these submarines will be withdrawn from service as required to permit the introduction of additional Ohio Class submarines. The 12 Franklin and Madison Class SSBNs with Trident I C4 missiles are scheduled to remain in service until the turn of the century. Trident I missiles could potentially carry as many as 10 warheads of 100-kt yield but the practice is to carry 8 warheads. This represents not only a doubling of the yield of Poseidon missile warheads, but also a considerable increase in missile accuracy through the use of stellar-inertial guidance corrections to missiles in flight. (Missiles carry equipment that takes a position fix based on star locations and then makes necessary corrections to the missile's course.) Although not widely known, the Trident I missile has proved far more accurate than planned—perhaps accurate enough to obviate the 'requirement' for the Trident II missile.[13]

Trident II missiles will have greatly increased accuracy (reportedly 400 feet) compared to previous SLBMs.[14] This is to be achieved by a combination of improved submarine navigation (it is essential to know as precisely as possible a submarine's firing location in order to assure accuracy) and missile navigation systems. In contrast to the general perception that increased missile accuracy has led to smaller warhead yields, the D5 warhead—the W87—will have a yield of some 475 kt, a tenfold increase from the Poseidon W68 warhead. The combination of improved accuracy and very high yield will give the D5 its counterforce capability. Depending on arms control results, deploying the D5 would then add between 3840 and 7200 counterforce warheads to the US strategic arsenal (almost four to seven times the number on ICBMs in mid-1987), depending on the number of submarines eventually built and on whether they carry 8 or 12 warheads or some combination thereof. The US Department of Defense (DoD) has indicated that it wants 20 Trident submarines and perhaps as many as 25. However, according to the DoD, the 'force-level goal for strategic submarines has not been determined; the eventual force level will depend on arms reduction talks and other factors'.[15] In December 1987, the USA and the USSR agreed on the 'counting rules' to be used in the START negotiations. The USA declared that it will deploy no more than eight warheads on the Trident II missile.[16] This represents a departure from the position advocated by prominent defence officials to test and deploy up to 12 warheads per missile.

US strategic submarines operate in the Atlantic and Pacific Oceans. All 28 pre-Ohio Class submarines operate from bases in the Atlantic: from Charleston, South Carolina and King's Bay, Georgia on the US East Coast and forward deployed from Holy Loch, Scotland. King's Bay has been chosen as the base for the second squadron of Ohio Class submarines, all of which will carry the Trident II D5 missile, starting in 1989. The first squadron of eight Ohio Class submarines is assigned to Bangor, Washington, and all eight are operating in the Pacific Ocean.

All US strategic submarines have two crews—one Blue and one Gold—which take alternate patrols and training periods. Patrols take 70 days with roughly 25 days in between for resupply and maintenance.

British strategic submarines

The United Kingdom operates a force of four Resolution Class SSBNs that are each equipped with 16 modernized Polaris A3 missiles (see table 21). The Polaris missiles have each recently received a new 'front end' called Chevaline, which includes new warheads, a guidance package and other features to improve their ability to reach their targets by various means. Each missile, designated A3-TK, carries two multiple re-entry vehicle (MRV) warheads that can strike only one target, and also carries so-called 'penetration aids' (decoys, chaff, etc.) designed to fool anti-ballistic missile (ABM) systems. The Chevaline programme, which began in 1974 and was completed in mid-1987, has improved the accuracy, range and operational flexibility of Britain's strategic submarine force, especially in order to get past the modernized Moscow ABM system.

Table 21. British, French and Chinese strategic submarine forces— 1988

Number and class of submarine	First year deployed	Number and type of missile	Range (km)	Warheads x yield	Warheads deployed
UK					
4 Resolution	1968/ 1982[a]	16 x Polaris A3TK	4700	2 x 40 kt (MRV)	128
France					
4 Redoutable	1972	16 x M20	3000	1 x 3 Mt	64
1 Redoutable	1987[b]	16 x M4 (mod)	6000	4-6 x 150 kt	96
1 Invincible	1985	16 x M4A	4-5000	6 x 150 kt	96
China					
1 Golf[c]	1964	2 x CSS-N-3	3300	1 x .0.2-1 Mt	0
2 Xia	1983	12 x CSS-N-3	3300	1 x .0.2-1 Mt	24
Totals					
13		*186*			*408*

[a] The Polaris A3TK missiles were first deployed in 1982, although the Resolution Class began operating with the Polaris A3 in 1968.

[b] This submarine was converted to carry modified M4 missiles in 1987, although it had previously carried M20 missiles.

[c] This is a test and training submarine that is assumed not to be armed in peacetime, although it could be during a crisis.

Sources: See table 12.

Of the four submarines, one or two are usually on patrol, with a third in port and the fourth undergoing maintenance or refit and thus being out of service.[17] The submarines are assigned to a home port at Faslane on the Clyde Estuary in Scotland, near the US submarine base at Holy Loch. Each submarine has two crews which rotate on 12-week cycles: 4 weeks of trials and maintenance, and 8 weeks on patrol. These submarines are usually under the operational control of the North Atlantic Treaty Organization (NATO) and are assigned targets accordingly, although the UK could use the submarines unilaterally if it were a matter of 'supreme national interest'. It is believed that the British SSBNs operate west of Ireland, close enough to home to permit British aircraft to observe their patrol areas and protect the submarines there.

In 1986 the keel of the first of a new class of British SSBNs was laid, the first step in Britain's most ambitious and expensive nuclear weapon acquisition plan to date. The first submarine will be called the *Vanguard*, and there are plans to build four of the Vanguard Class SSBNs to carry up to 512 accurate MIRVed warheads on Trident II/D5 missiles which are to be purchased from the USA. This would represent an eightfold increase in the number of targets that Britain's submarines could attack, compared to the current possibility of 64 targets. It will also mean the UK could attack any type of target it chooses, including hardened military command sites or missile silos. Each submarine will have 16 tubes for Trident II SLBMs, each of which will carry as many as 8 British-designed and built warheads. The *Vanguard* is scheduled to enter service in the mid- to late 1990s, but the programme to build four will not be completed before the year 2000.[18]

The current inventory of Polaris A3-TK missiles (with the Chevaline upgrade) had engines that were originally built in 1967-68. In order to allow the missiles to keep working through the 1990s (until they are replaced by the Trident force) the engines needed to be replaced. New engines were scheduled to have been installed as of mid-1987.

French strategic submarines

France has operated ballistic missile submarines since 1972 and is now in the midst of a major modernization programme for its SSBN/ SLBM force. Six submarines comprise the French Force Océanique Stratégique (FOST): five Redoutable Class SSBNs dating from the early 1970s and a new SSBN (*l'Inflexible*, the only one of its class) that began operating in April 1985. The five Redoutable Class submarines were originally all equipped with 16 M20 SLBMs, each of which had a single 1-Mt warhead. In 1985 France deployed a new SLBM, the M4, on its newest submarine, *l'Inflexible*. The M4 missile can carry as many as six MIRVed warheads with a yield of 150 kt and is designed to penetrate the Moscow ABM system. Four of the Redoutable Class submarines, excluding the *Redoutable* itself, are planned to have M4 missiles installed (or 'backfitted') to replace their M20 SLBMs by 1992. Thus the French FOST is in the process of transformation from a force carrying 80 warheads to one carrying as many as 496 MIRVed warheads (480 M4, plus 16 M20), more than a sixfold increase in the number of targets France could attack (see table 21).

In addition to the new M4 missiles being installed in most of the French SSBNs, France has made improvements to the warheads for the M4. The original warhead was the TN-70, 96 of which have been installed on *l'Inflexible*. A new warhead known as the TN-71 is smaller and lighter than the TN-70 and is reportedly better able to penetrate ABM defences. In 1985 the last of the Redoutable Class SSBNs, the *Tonnant*, was removed from service in order to have M4 missiles installed. The refit was completed by late 1987 with TN-71 warheads on M4 missiles. A test launch of the M4 with a TN-71 warhead package took place in March 1986 and demonstrated a range of 6000 km, some 2000 km longer than that of the TN-70-equipped missiles. Eventually all M4 SLBMs are expected to be fitted with TN-71 warheads.

Beyond these programmes to modernize its strategic submarine forces, France is also planning to introduce another new model of SSBN in 1994, the seventh in its planned fleet. This 'new generation' (NG) submarine was expected to be ordered in early 1987 and would be both quieter and capable of diving deeper than existing French SSBNs.[19] Yet another warhead is planned for the NG submarine—the TN-75 model to be installed on M4 SLBMs. The M4 missiles, too, will be replaced on the NG submarine before the end of the century by new M5 missiles that will each have 8-12 warheads of the new TN-76 design. Each of the warheads will reportedly be lighter, more compact and less visible to ABM radar than the previous ones.[20] They will also have more ability to evade ballistic missile defences and to destroy hardened targets, such as missile sites and command posts.

Thus, France is undertaking an across-the-board modernization programme of all elements of its strategic submarine forces, including the communication systems. These complicated plans were outlined in the five-year military budget law in France in 1986. It is conceivable that future budget decisions will change the plans.

France operates three submarines at sea at all times and has a policy of having four SSBNs available for immediate operations. Even during the M4 refit period there will be four SSBNs available through careful scheduling. Each submarine has two crews that alternate on two-month patrols, believed to be in the eastern Atlantic off the coasts of France or Portugal. The submarines are based at Ile Longue near Brest from which they have easy access to the open sea.

Chinese strategic submarines

China is the most recent member of the SLBM club and also the smallest. It embarked on a ballistic missile submarine programme as the last element of its strategic forces, after land-based ballistic missiles and bombers. Since China possesses no more than 200 ballistic missiles on land (probably closer to 150), the importance of strategic submarines is heightened as its least vulnerable retaliatory force. There are three strategic submarines known to be in the Chinese Navy: two Xia Class SSBNs that have been launched since 1981 and one Golf Class SSB that has been used as a test launch vessel. The Golf Class submarine has two modified missile tubes in its sail structure, but is thought to be used only for crew training and missile testing and not normally deployed with operational missiles. (It is possible that the submarine could be equipped with working SLBMs in a time of crisis.) Two Xia Class submarines are at sea with 12 CSS-N-3 SLBMs each. The CSS-N-3 carries a single warhead believed to be between 200 and 1000 kt in yield (see table 21). With a maximum range of 3300 km it could strike targets throughout Soviet Asia as well as the surrounding Pacific region.

The Xia Class submarines and their CSS-N-3 missiles represent China's longest and most difficult nuclear weapon development programme; these systems have been in various stages of development for over 15 years. One Xia Class SSBN has been declared operational by the Chinese Government, although in an indirect manner. In January 1987, it produced a photograph of the submarine clearly showing its 12 missile hatches and saying that it had begun operations.[21]

Since the Chinese Government does not discuss publicly the details of its current nuclear weapons, one must rely upon other sources of information as well as Chinese practice. Several additional Xia Class SSBNs are under construction, and it is estimated that China plans to build between six and eight for the total programme. In missile tests during 1985 and 1986 China reportedly made progress towards MIRV technologies for its ballistic missiles, and increases in missile range and accuracy. At least one test involved an SLBM launch, for which Deng Xiaoping, Chairman of the Central Military Commission (and paramount leader of China), commended the test personnel.[22] If China proceeds with a MIRV programme, it would allow an expansion of the nuclear arsenal without necessarily increasing the number of missiles or launchers. It would also complicate any adversary's attempt to defend against Chinese missiles with a ballistic missile defence system.

Summary and conclusions

It is clear that strategic submarine forces play an increasingly important central role in the nuclear arms race. Considerable national resources are being invested by all five nuclear weapon states to modernize and expand their SSBN and SLBM arsenals. There is also a growing interest in ASW as submarine forces become more capable and threatening. Only two nations—the USA and the USSR—have any (though limited) arms control restraints on their strategic submarine forces. The other three nations are proceeding with SSBN/SLBM programmes that will fundamentally change their positions in the nuclear competition. They will have accurate missiles with hundreds of warheads that cannot be ignored by their adversaries or by arms control negotiators. If the two superpowers do reach agreement on substantial cuts in their strategic nuclear weapon arsenals, it would reduce their strategic submarine forces towards the size of the other three. It would then be even more important to include the other growing nuclear weapon nations in future arms control considerations.

IV. Non-strategic naval nuclear forces

Those naval nuclear weapons which are not SSBNs and SLBMs are called either non-strategic or tactical, and occasionally theatre, weapons. (Although the terms 'non-strategic' and 'tactical' are somewhat interchangeable, the former is broader and better suited to include all systems.) The distinctions between strategic and non-strategic weapons are in many ways artificial; they pertain mostly to weapon system ranges and whether plans have been made to include a given weapon in central nuclear war plans. For arms control purposes the essential distinction is that strategic systems are included in arms control talks and agreements, where the USA and the USSR have agreed on the definition of 'strategic'; whereas tactical ones are not.

A full explanation of the terms 'strategic' and 'tactical' would probably include the distinction that strategic systems are those which are carried by long-range launchers, generally of intercontinental range (more than 5500 km), and for which targets have been planned ahead (or preplanned) as part of central nuclear war plans. Tactical systems have ranges that require them to be present in or near the theatre in which they would be used (hence the term 'theatre nuclear forces', or TNF) and are generally considered unsuitable for preplanning because their use depends entirely on a crisis or war as it unfolds. In the case of land-attack weapons the emphasis on nuclear-armed SLCMs is blurring the distinction between strategic and non-strategic weapons: these SLCMs clearly have attributes of both types, but do not fit into any neat category. The US Navy assigns strategic, theatre and reserve roles to its SLCMs. Some SLCMs are assigned preplanned targets but they would not necessarily be launched under the central US nuclear war plan, the Single Integrated Operational Plan (SIOP). The same may be true for Soviet SLCMs.

Non-strategic nuclear weapons can be divided into two general categories: land-attack weapons and weapons for warfare at sea. The general naval terms for these two categories are 'power projection' (or strike warfare) for the former and 'sea control' for the latter. These terms pertain to naval attacks against land targets and against targets at sea, respectively.

Power projection is the term used to describe naval attacks against land targets. It includes everything from amphibious invasions to shore bombardment with naval gunfire, and nuclear attacks with carrier-based aircraft or SLCMs. Land-attack nuclear weapons are comprised primarily of nuclear-capable aircraft carrying bombs and also of cruise missiles.

This form of naval warfare is becoming increasingly important for several reasons. First, naval warfare probably could not be confined to the seas alone; it would almost certainly be part of a larger war. In such a war, attacks would inevitably be made against targets on land, such as ships and submarines in naval ports or harbours, air bases where naval aircraft are or might be stationed, command or communication centres, and supply depots for naval equipment. Additionally, some naval nuclear weapons are stored at land depots and air bases, as are US B57 depth bombs for ASW or Soviet air-to-surface anti-ship cruise missiles, creating an important set of nuclear targets. The two superpower navies are increasing their abilities to attack other nations from the seas, which almost amounts to an extension of their strategic submarine mission. These forces will become more important as their targets become increasingly important and as strategic nuclear forces, including SSBNs/SLBMs, become subject to the possibility of considerable reduction from arms control agreements, thereby prompting military planners to seek alternative means of striking at existing targets. In addition, non-ballistic nuclear missile systems may become of greater interest to the nuclear weapon nations if ballistic missile defence (BMD) systems are developed and deployed further by any nation, most likely by the USA under its Strategic Defense Initiative (SDI), and by the USSR under its modernized and expanded Moscow ABM system.

Sea control is the term for those actions which assure that a navy has unobstructed use of an ocean area, including fighting and destroying adversary naval forces at sea: ships, submarines and aircraft, and their weapons. (See the discussion of command of the sea in part I, chapter 2 on force comparison.) Sea control entails three separate types of warfare for the three components of naval forces: anti-surface warfare (ASUW) against ships, anti-submarine warfare (ASW) and anti-air warfare (AAW) against aerial targets such as aircraft and cruise missiles. With one major exception, these three forms of warfare would be fought at sea, as distinct from against land targets.

In naval warfare there is a great premium on attacking adversary forces before they have a chance to attack. The Soviet Navy is thought to rely upon this condition, often called the 'struggle for the first salvo', in an effort to compensate for and overwhelm its superior opponent. The US Navy is increasing its ability to destroy Soviet naval units before they can be used. According to former US Defense Secretary Caspar Weinberger: 'Naval modernization programs emphasize the development of weapons and tactics that allow our forces—once hostilities have been initiated—to strike first from extended ranges. The approach emphasizes surveillance systems capable of detecting enemy forces at long ranges, well before our own forces can be targeted.'[23] Since the superpower navies would prefer to destroy naval targets before they could be used, nominally sea control missions (ASUW, ASW and AAW) could take place against their respective targets at their land bases in an effort to destroy ships and submarines in port or aircraft at their bases. Referring to Soviet tactical naval missiles, Weinberger stated: '...because they are difficult to intercept, the missiles can best be countered by detecting and engaging the aircraft and vessels that carry them. In some instances, this may require long-range strikes against enemy bases in an effort to destroy bombers or naval vessels before they have an opportunity to inititate an air attack.'[24] Failing this dangerous pre-emptive effort, weapons for war at sea would indeed be used *at sea*.

Nuclear weapons for warfare at sea include torpedoes and depth bombs (rocket-propelled or dropped by aircraft) for ASW, sub-surface-, surface- and air-launched cruise missiles and gravity bombs for destroying ships, and surface-to-air missiles for AAW. Some systems can be used for more than one type of target. For example, nuclear gravity bombs could be used either for land-attack or for attacking ships at sea. Likewise, nuclear anti-ship cruise missiles (ASCMs) could be used to attack land targets.

Non-strategic naval nuclear arsenals

Four nations are estimated to possess a combined total of more than 6500 non-strategic naval nuclear weapons: the USSR, the USA, the UK and France (see table 22). The USSR has the greatest variety of weapons deployed (more than 20 types) on more than 45 types of vessel: ships, submarines and aircraft. In all, there are estimated to be more than 2700 Soviet non-strategic nuclear warheads. The USA has the greatest quantity of weapons (some 3600), also spread throughout its naval vessels: 25 classes of ships and submarines (as well as the support and logistics ships that can carry weapons) and 8 types of air-craft. The UK operates 3 aircraft carriers with nuclear-capable attack jets and 20 other surface ships that carry nuclear-capable helicopters for ASW, for a total of some 170 warheads. France maintains two aircraft carriers with 36 nuclear-capable bombers and their nuclear gravity bombs. A detailed description of these four nations' non-strategic naval nuclear forces follows.

Table 22. Non-strategic naval nuclear weapons—1988

	USA	USSR	UK	France	Total
Aircraft bombs	1450	0[a]	34	36	*1520*
Land-attack SLCMs	150	12	0	0	*162*
Anti-ship weapons	0	948	0	0	*948*
ASW weapons	1760	1401	134	0	*3295*
Anti-air weapons	285	260	0	0	*545*
Artillery	0	100	0	0	*100*
Totals	*3645*	*2721*	*168*	*36*	*6570*

[a]The number of nuclear bombs deployed for Soviet naval aircraft is unknown; there could be many hundreds.

Sources: See table 12.

Soviet non-strategic naval nuclear forces

The Soviet Navy is fundamentally a nuclear navy that has invested heavily in nuclear weapons at the expense of conventional ones. This may be partly because of its perceived inability to defeat its stronger adversary with conventional weapons. It has by far the greatest variety of non-strategic nuclear weapons of any nation. More than 2700 nuclear weapons have been integrated into all components of the navy: ships, submarines and naval aviation. These weapons are available for all types of naval warfare: land attack and the three types of warfare at sea—ASUW, ASW and AAW. In addition to shorter-range Soviet SLBMs, according to the US DoD:

The Soviet Navy also maintains an extensive sea-based non-strategic nuclear force comprising both antisurface warfare (ASUW) and antisubmarine warfare (ASW) as well as land-attack systems. The Soviets maintain an inventory of nuclear-armed torpedoes as well as ASW depth bombs; the newest versions of both entered service in the early 1980s. The Soviet Navy also deploys an extensive array of ASUW and ASW cruise missile systems, ranging from the SS-N-3 to the newer SS-N-19 and SS-N-22; the latter two were also introduced in the early 1980s.[25]

Over 90 per cent of Soviet major surface combatants are estimated to carry at least one weapon system that can use nuclear warheads. Virtually all submarines are nuclear-capable (consider the Soviet Whiskey Class submarine stranded in Swedish territorial waters in 1981 that was determined by Swedish Government authorities to be carrying nuclear-armed torpedoes), and most of the Soviet Naval Aviation (SNA) aircraft can carry nuclear or nuclear-capable weapons.

All of the different types of Soviet naval weapon are believed to have a nuclear capability, from torpedoes to gravity bombs and depth charges, and to cruise missiles and ballistic missiles. Nuclear-capable systems are deployed on a wide variety of vessels, from the largest V/STOL aircraft carriers to patrol combatants, and to submarines and aircraft, new and old. However, the supply of nuclear warheads deployed at sea with these forces is estimated to be such (warheads are deployed only for systems on launchers—with no reloads available on most vessels) that they could best be used in a one-shot manner.[26] Given the limited supplies of ammunition available on most ships, the problem can be posed this way: What will the Soviet Navy vessels do when they run out of conventional ammunition in a war, use nuclear weapons or risk being destroyed while retreating to reload more weapons?

Power projection/ land attack. The Soviet Navy traditionally has not concentrated on power projection capabilities, but has instead focused on protecting its territory and naval forces from naval attack. Consequently, there has been little emphasis on or requirement for land-attack systems for naval warfare—aside from strategic submarines. Soviet naval nuclear land-attack capabilities reside almost entirely in its strategic submarine force, including 12 Golf II Class SSBs that carry intermediate-range (1400 km) SLBMs assigned to theatre roles in Europe and in the Pacific (i.e., not against US territory). Other SSBNs, particularly of the Yankee I Class which carry SLBMs of less than intercontinental range, may be assigned to targets other than in the continental USA, especially against nuclear targets in Europe and Asia. This is all the more likely as a possible means of compensating for those nuclear missiles to be eliminated under the terms of the INF Treaty.

But in addition to its SLBMs, the Soviet Navy has been developing nuclear SLCMs for land-attack missions, and began to operate the first of two such missiles—the SS-N-21—in 1987.[27] The SS-N-21

Sampson SLCM was first placed aboard a former Yankee Class SSBN that has been converted especially to carry the missile.[28] This newest SLCM is small enough to be fired from standard 533-mm torpedo tubes, making it potentially available to a large portion of the Soviet submarine fleet, depending on their fire control and targeting capabilities. The US DoD estimates that the most likely launch platforms for the missile are the Akula, Sierra and Victor III Classes. The nuclear-only SS-N-21 has a range of 3000 km and may have a warhead yield of some 200 kt. It is the naval variant of the AS-15 Kent air-launched cruise missile (ALCM) and the SSC-X-4 ground-launched cruise missile (GLCM) that was developed before being banned by the INF Treaty.

The second model of Soviet nuclear land-attack SLCM is the supersonic SS-NX-24 which has been under development for several years. It is much larger than the SS-N-21, measuring more than 12 metres in length and having a wing span wider than 5 metres, and would require a specially configured submarine to launch it.[29] Flight tests have been conducted from a converted former Yankee Class SSBN, and more such tests are expected in 1988. Given the missile's large size (larger than some SLBMs) and special launcher requirements, it is not clear that it will be produced in large numbers, perhaps only for converted Yankee Class submarines removed from ballistic missile duty. Furthermore, the USA and the USSR began discussions in late 1987 to find some means of limiting nuclear SLCMs, thus casting further doubt on the eventual role of the SS-NX-24.

Many of the six different types of nuclear-capable cruise missile that are available for anti-ship purposes, especially against US aircraft carrier battle groups, could also be used in a secondary role to attack certain land targets, such as ports, naval bases, and command, control, communications and intelligence (C^3I) facilities near coastal areas, depending on the missile's range, launch, flight, navigation and guidance characteristics. Although older missile systems, such as the SS-N-3 and the SS-N-7, have limitations or drawbacks that make them unsuitable for land attacks, newer ones, such as SS-N-12 missiles deployed on modified Echo II Class nuclear-powered cruise missile submarines (SSGNs) and SS-N-19 missiles deployed on Oscar Class SSGNs, are better suited to attacking land targets (see table 23). US military planners have occasionally expressed worries about potential Soviet abilities to launch surprise attacks against US coastal targets from forward deployed conventionally powered cruise missile submarines (SSGs) and

SSGNs—as well as from nearby SSBs and SSBNs—as part of a sudden nuclear first strike.

Table 23. Soviet nuclear-capable anti-ship cruise missiles (ASCMs) —1988

Weapon type	Number deployed	First year deployed	Range (km)	Warhead x yield	Warheads deployed	Platform
SLCMs						
SS-N-3a/c	148	1960	460	1 x 350 kt	104	Echo II, Juliett
SS-N-3b	80	1960	460	1 x 350 kt	16	Kresta I, Kynda
SS-N-7	90	1968	65	1 x 200 kt	44	Charlie I, Papa
SS-N-9	208	1969	280	1 x 200 kt	78	Charlie II, Papa, Nanuchka, Sarancha
SS-N-12	200	1976	550	1 x 350 kt	76	Kiev, Slava, Echo II
SS-N-19	136	1980	550	1 x 500 kt	56	Kirov, Oscar
SS-N-22	80	1981	100	1 x 200 kt	24	Sovremennyy, Tarantul III
Coastal Missiles						
SSC-1b	100	1962	450	1 x 50-200 kt	100	land-based
ASMs					450[a]	
AS-2	-	1961	185-210	1		Badger
AS-4	-	1967	280-560	1		Backfire B/C
AS-5	-	1965	180-220	1		Badger C/G
AS-6	-	1970	280-460	1		Badger/G, Backfire B/C

[a]This is the number of nuclear-armed missiles of all four models estimated to be deployed for the force of naval strike aircraft.

Sources: See table 12.

One other variety of naval nuclear weapon may exist for power projection: nuclear artillery shells for old Soviet gunboats. Sverdlov Class cruisers have 152-mm guns that are presumed to be capable of firing the standard Soviet 152-mm nuclear artillery rounds. It is not known whether these old ships are nuclear-certified, nor how long they will stay in service. Given the other manifold Soviet nuclear capabilities, it seems questionable whether the Soviet Navy would bother training, certifying or arming Sverdlov Class ships with nuclear artillery shells.[30] Nevertheless, such logic seldom prevents the deployment of dubious nuclear weapon systems, and it is estimated that 100 nuclear artillery shells have been stockpiled for Sverdlovs.[31]

Sea control/sea denial. For sea control missions (often called 'sea denial' for the USSR since it is considered incapable of achieving sea control against the USA and thus having the countermission to US sea control), the USSR deploys more than 20 types of nuclear weapon aboard 29 classes of ship, 23 classes of submarine and at least 7 types of aircraft for all three tasks (see table 24). Of 810 naval vessels, comprising major surface warships, submarines and patrol combatants, some 660 (more than 80 per cent) are assumed by the US DoD to be nuclear-capable. Although the Soviet Union has no ship-borne nuclear-capable fixed-wing aircraft (some ASW helicopters are presumed to have nuclear ASW missions), nearly 700 land-based aircraft assigned to naval aviation are available for nuclear strikes against surface and submarine forces within range of their land bases. According to the US DoD, all Soviet air-launched ASCMs are nuclear-capable, as are those ASCMs launched by submarines.[32]

In order to combat US surface, submarine and air forces at sea, the Soviet Navy operates a large number of submarines, land-based aircraft and ships armed with sea control weapons, many of them nuclear or nuclear-capable. Submarines provide the Soviet Navy with its most powerful sea control/sea denial capabilities. The Soviet submarine fleet is the largest in the world and includes attack and cruise missile submarines that have anti-submarine and anti-ship missions, respectively.

ASUW. Given the considerable offensive capabilities of the US surface fleet, ASUW is a high priority for the Soviet Navy, particularly in waters around and approaching Soviet territory. Some 63 cruise missile submarines of six types (49 SSGNs and 14 SSGs), all of which are thought to be nuclear-capable, have the mission of attacking US surface ships, particularly aircraft carrier battle groups. According to US defence officials: 'A major concern of all four [Soviet] fleets would be countering Western naval strike groups, especially aircraft carriers and cruise missile platforms approaching the USSR.'[33] Five different types of nuclear-capable ASCM are deployed aboard Soviet submarines: SS-N-3, SS-N-7, SS-N-9, SS-N-12 and SS-N-19 (see table 23). Old SS-N-3 missiles are being replaced by the SS-N-12 model on some Echo II Class SSGNs. Many of these and other nuclear ASCMs are also deployed on 10 classes of surface ship, thus providing the USSR with a large variety and number of vessels for nuclear attacks against ships.

Table 24. Soviet non-strategic naval nuclear weapons—1988

Weapon type	Carrier platform
Land-attack weapons	
SS-N-21	Yankee, (Victor III, Sierra, Akula)[a]
SS-NX-24	Yankee[b]
Artillery shells[c]	Sverdlov
Anti-ship weapons	
SS-N-3a/c	Echo II, Juliett
SS-N-3b	Kresta I, Kynda
SS-N-7	Charlie I, Papa
SS-N-9	Charlie II, Papa, Nanuchka, Sarancha
SS-N-12	Kiev, Slava, Echo II
SS-N-19	Kirov, Oscar
SS-N-22	Sovremennyy, Tarantul III
SSC-1b	Land-based coastal missile
AS-2	Badger C
AS-4	Backfire B/C
AS-5	Badger C/G
AS-6	Badger C/G, Backfire B/C
ASW weapons	
SS-N-15	Typhoon, Charlie I/II, Papa, Oscar, Victor I/II/III, Alfa, Sierra, Mike, Akula, Romeo[d],Tango[d]
SS-N-16	Typhoon, Oscar, Sierra, Mike, Akula, Victor II/III
FRAS-1	Kiev, Moskva
Torpedoes[e]	Virtually all submarines; most ships
Depth bombs	Bear F, Mail, May, Helix A, Hormone A
Anti-air weapons	
SA-N-1	Kresta I, Kynda, Kanin, Kashin, Mod. Kashin, SAM Kotlin
SA-N-3	Moskva, Kiev, Kresta II, Kara
SA-N-6	Kirov, Slava, Kara (1)

[a] The SS-N-21 is operational on a converted Yankee SSGN; the Akula, Sierra and Victor III are considered the most likely future carriers.

[b] The SS-NX-24 has been flight-tested from a converted Yankee submarine and is expected to be operational in 1988-89.

[c] These could also be used against other naval vessels.

[d] Possible SS-N-15 platform.

[e] The US Joint Chiefs of Staff have identified two nuclear-armed torpedoes: the Type 65 and the ET-80.

Sources: See table 12.

The third branch of Soviet ASUW forces are the aircraft assigned to SNA. Soviet nuclear-capable naval aircraft for anti-ship duties are all land-based and thus able to operate within only a limited radius from the USSR. This accords well with the Soviet priority of protecting its home territory, its SSBNs and the sea approaches to the USSR against naval attack, meaning relatively close to home and within range of its land-based aircraft. The main aircraft operated by SNA for ASUW missions are the 143 Backfire and 240 Badger bombers which can carry four models of air-to-surface ASCMs, the AS-2, AS-4, AS-5 and AS-6, all of which are nuclear-capable (see table 23).

The US Navy has stated that it considers SNA aircraft, particularly Backfire and Badger bombers, carrying ASCMs to be one of the most dangerous challenges to US surface ships. Former Defense Secretary Caspar Weinberger stated that US nuclear AAW weapons are meant to deter attacks 'by Soviet nuclear antiship missiles (especially those aboard Backfire and Badger bombers)'.[34] This is one of the justifications made for new US nuclear AAW weapon requests, such as the Standard Missile 2.

In addition to these nuclear ASUW forces, the Soviet Union also has one model of land-based ASCM—the SSC-1b—which is nuclear-capable. It is estimated that 100 nuclear warheads for the former missiles are deployed.[35] The SSC-1b missiles have a range of approximately 450 km and a yield believed to be between 50 and 200 kt.[36]

ASW. For anti-submarine warfare (ASW), the USSR has nuclear weapons available on submarines, ships and aircraft. Virtually all Soviet submarines are equipped with standard 533-mm torpedo tubes which make them capable of carrying and using nuclear torpedoes of the same diameter; however, not all submarines are necessarily armed with nuclear torpedoes. The US JCS have identified two Soviet nuclear-armed torpedoes as the Type 65 and the ET-80.[37] Many surface ships also carry the standard 533-mm torpedoes, with almost 250 nuclear versions estimated to be so deployed.[38] It is possible that the Soviet Navy has also built nuclear-capable torpedoes for aerial delivery. If this is true, then almost any SNA aircraft with sufficient lift capacity could be equipped with such air-launched nuclear torpedoes. This would overcome the major disadvantage of nuclear torpedoes fired from submarines or ships: their relatively short range could put the launching vessel at risk from the effects of the nuclear explosion. This is one of the reasons that the USA abandoned its ASTOR (*anti-*

*s*ubmarine *tor*pedo) nuclear torpedo programme and developed a torpedo that combined the flight and range characteristics of a guided missile with a torpedo, called SUBROC (*sub*marine *roc*ket).

Two other nuclear weapon systems can also be fired from standard torpedo tubes: the SS-N-15 nuclear depth bomb similar to the US SUBROC system and the SS-N-16 ASW missile carrying a homing torpedo. The SS-N-16 is a later modification of the SS-N-15, carrying a nuclear-capable homing torpedo instead of a nuclear depth bomb. It is possible that the SS-N-16 requires a 650-mm torpedo tube, but both missile systems are often considered to be on the same submarines. Nearly 400 of these two similar systems are believed to be variously deployed on 13 classes of submarine, including the most recent attack submarine classes (Akula and Sierra) and Typhoon Class SSBNs (see table 24).

Nuclear depth bombs are common ASW weapons. They can be fired from torpedo tubes, as in the SS-N-15, or they can be dropped by aircraft. The Soviet Navy possesses an estimated 280 nuclear depth bombs for land-based and ship-based aircraft. The land-based aircraft comprise some 55 Bear F, 96 Be-12 Mail and some 50 Il-38 May maritime patrol aircraft, and two models of helicopter—140 Ka-25 Hormone A and 50 Ka-27 Helix (some of which are based on ships)—which are credited with a nuclear depth bomb capability. One other ship-borne nuclear system is the FRAS-1 (for *f*ree *r*ocket, *a*nti-*s*ubmarine) rocket-delivered depth bomb, also referred to as SUW-N-1 (the launcher designation), some 25 of which are deployed on Moskva and Kiev Class aircraft carriers. With a range of some 30 km, the FRAS-1 is best suited to protect Soviet anti-carrier forces from Western attack submarines.

It has sometimes been suggested that the Soviet Navy has built nuclear mines for use against both ships and submarines.[39] There is no official Western corroboration of this suggestion, and their use would seem to run strongly against logic: they cannot be targeted on specific and known targets; they are by their nature indiscriminate; and they could destroy the wrong vessel in a war. Nor can they be easily and positively controlled by central Soviet civilian leaders—presumably an essential condition for Soviet nuclear forces. It is, therefore, doubtful whether the USSR has indeed built and deployed these systems on an operational basis, if at all.

AAW. Although the US Navy does not have nuclear weapons designed exclusively for striking Soviet surface ships, the Soviet Navy has deployed a considerable force of nuclear anti-air missiles. These would be available to counter US aircraft and missiles. Some 260 nuclear AAW weapons are estimated to be deployed on 11 classes of surface ships, including aircraft carriers, cruisers and destroyers (see table 25). There are three models of surface-to-air missiles (SAMs) credited with a nuclear capability—the SA-N-1, the SA-N-3 and the SA-N-6. A fourth model—the SA-N-2—may have been nuclear-capable, but is believed to be retired.

Table 25. Soviet naval nuclear-capable AAW forces—1988

Missile type	Number deployed[a]	First year deployed	Range (km)	Warhead x yield	Nuclear warheads deployed	Platform
SA-N-1	1112	1961	22	1 x 10 kt	152	Kresta I, Kynda, Kanin,Kashin, Mod. Kashin, SAM Kotlin
SA-N-3	1600	1967	37	1 x 10 kt	92	Moskva, Kiev, Kresta II, Kara
SA-N-6	320	1981	65	1 x 10 kt	16	Kirov, Slava, Kara[b]

[a]These are missiles deployed on launchers.
[b]Only one Kara Class cruiser is equipped with the SA-N-6 system.

Sources: See table 12.

US non-strategic naval nuclear weapons

It is sometimes said that the US Navy is the world's third largest nuclear weapon power. It possesses almost 9300 nuclear weapons, of which nearly 3700 are non-strategic, more than the other nuclear navies combined. Eight models of nuclear weapons are deployed for some 312 ships and submarines of 33 classes and for more than 1700 naval aircraft of 8 models (see tables 26 and 27). These nuclear and nuclear-capable forces serve a range of missions and roles from power projection/land attack to sea control and the tasks of ASW and AAW.

Table 26.   US nuclear-capable naval vessels—1988

Class	Number deployed	Nuclear weapons
Strategic submarines		
Lafayette	8	Poseidon C3
Madison	8	Poseidon C3/Trident I C4
Franklin	12	Poseidon C3/Trident I C4
Ohio	8	Trident I C4
	36	
Attack submarines		
Los Angeles	37	Tomahawk, SUBROC
Sturgeon	37	Tomahawk, SUBROC
Permit	13	SUBROC
Narwhal	1	SUBROC
Lipscomb	1	SUBROC
	89	
Aircraft carriers		(Bombs and nuclear depth bombs are on all carriers)
Midway	2	Bombs (B43, B57, B61), depth bombs (B57)
Forrestal	4	"
Kitty Hawk	2	"
John F. Kennedy	1	"
Enterprise	1	"
Nimitz	4	"
Tarawa[a]	5	Nuclear bombs and other Marine Corps nuclear weapons
	19	
Battleships		
Iowa	3	Tomahawk
Cruisers		
Ticonderoga	9	ASROC (CG-47—CG-51), Tomahawk (CG-52 and later)
Virginia	4	ASROC, Tomahawk
Truxtun	1	Terrier, ASROC
Bainbridge	1	Terrier, ASROC
Long Beach	1	Terrier, ASROC, Tomahawk
Belknap	9	Terrier, ASROC
Leahy	9	Terrier, ASROC
California	2	ASROC
	36	

Class	Number deployed	Nuclear weapons
Destroyers		
Spruance	31	ASROC, Tomahawk
Adams	23	ASROC
Farragut	10	ASROC, Terrier
	64	
Frigates		
Brooke	6	ASROC
Glover	1	ASROC
Knox	46	ASROC
Garcia	10	ASROC
Bronstein	2	ASROC
	65	
Submarines and ships		
Subtotal	*312*	
Attack aircraft		
A4M	110	B43, B57, B61 nuclear bombs
A-6E	279	"
A-7E	240	"
AV-8B	100	B61 nuclear bomb
F/A-18	400	B57, B61 nuclear bombs
	1129	
ASW aircraft		
P-3B/C	347	B57 nuclear depth bomb
S-3A/B	187	B57 nuclear depth bomb
SH-3D/H	128	B57 nuclear depth bomb
	662	
Total naval nuclear delivery platforms:	*2103*	

*a*Tarawa Class (LHA 1) amphibious assault ships are not considered aircraft carriers, but can operate with Marine Corps AV-8B V/STOL aircraft and nuclear bombs, and so are included in this table. They are more capable than the Soviet V/STOL carriers.

Sources: See table 12.

Table 27. US non-strategic naval nuclear weapons—1988

Weapon category and/or type	First year deployed	Range (km)	Warheads deployed	Platform
Bombs				
B43/B57/B61	1961	—	1450	A-4M, A-6E, A-7E, AV-8B, F/A-18
SLCMs				
Tomahawk	1984	2500	150	Iowa, Long Beach, Virginia, Ticonderoga, Spruance, Los Angeles, Sturgeon
ASW weapons				
ASROC	1961	1-10	575	All cruisers except later Ticonderoga, all destroyers, all frigates except Perry Class
SUBROC	1965	60	285	Los Angeles, Sturgeon, Permit, Narwhal, Lipscomb
B57	1963	—	900	P-3B/C, S-3A/B, SH-3D/H
SAMs				
Terrier	1956	47	285	Leahy, Belknap, Bainbridge, Truxtun, Long Beach, Farragut
Total			*3 645*	

Sources: See table 12.

According to the navy, its 'non-strategic warhead programs support requirements for strike warfare (ashore targets), anti-submarine warfare, anti-air warfare and Marine Corps battlefield weapons'.[40] Wherever the US Navy sails, nuclear weapons go.

Although more is known about US naval nuclear weapons than those of any other nuclear navy, the need for and purpose of non-strategic nuclear weapons in the navy are questionable and unclear. The US Navy is essentially a conventional navy with widespread nuclear weapon capabilities. (The exception is the ballistic missile submarine force which is neither non-strategic nor for naval warfare——see section III of this chapter). Although aircraft carriers provided the USA with an early capability to drop nuclear bombs on the Soviet Union, tactical nuclear weapons for warfare at sea have been essentially an afterthought to the navy, stemming from the 1950s, when conventional weapons were less capable and destructive than today, and when nuclearization meant prestige among the military services.[41]

But aside from acquiring the weapons and making most ships nuclear-capable, the navy has largely ignored all but two types of nuclear weapon integrated into its forces—sea-launched cruise missiles and ASW weapons. For these two types of weapon considerable thought and planning have taken place; for other types little serious consideration appears to have been given.[42] Nevertheless, since 1980 the navy has been trying to modernize its entire arsenal of non-strategic nuclear weapons, justified on the basis of a 'growing Soviet nuclear threat'. However, it has not had much success in Congress and has failed to obtain funding for these programmes.[43]

Power projection/land attack. The US Navy has invested tremendous resources in power projection capabilities, which are the strongest of any nation. The navy has, since World War II, relied on its aircraft carriers as its primary power projection force, as well as the core of its fleet. More recently, as power projection and land attack have become more important to the navy and to its current strategy, SLCMs have come to supplement and expand that mission.

The navy has 14 active aircraft carriers in service, four of them nuclear-powered, and is aiming for a goal of 15 carriers through the first quarter of the 21st century. The attack aircraft aboard these ships are able to fly conventional or nuclear bombs as far as 800 kilometres. There are some 1450 nuclear bombs of three designs deployed for the carrier aircraft and for marine corps aircraft—the B43, B57 and B61 bombs—ranging in yield from about 5 kt to more than 1000 kt. This permits an average of about 100 bombs per carrier. These gravity bombs can be used against ships as well as against land targets.

Each carrier has a mixed group of aircraft, called the air wing, that is somewhat standard although the exact composition can vary. Carrier air wings typically consist of 86 aircraft, of which some 34 are nuclear-capable attack aircraft, and 16 are nuclear-capable ASW aircraft and helicopters (see table 1 in part I, chapter 2). All 14 carriers store nuclear bombs for their attack aircraft, of which there are three models—the A-6, A-7 and F/A-18. In addition, the US Marine Corps, which is within the Department of the Navy, operates three types of nuclear-capable aircraft—the AV-8B, A-4 and A-6. Five Tarawa Class amphibious assault ships (LHAs) can carry nuclear bombs for the AV-8B V/STOL aircraft they can carry. These LHAs are at least as capable as Soviet V/STOL ships; thus they are included in some totals of US aircraft carriers.

The nuclear power projection role of the aircraft carriers is to bomb land targets. Aircraft carriers were among the first US systems with a mission and capability to drop nuclear bombs on the Soviet Union, and they are still considered capable of being used for 'strategic' attacks.[44] The US Marine Corps also has a nuclear power projection mission, with nuclear artillery. Marine Corps assault units have 203-mm and 155-mm nuclear-capable systems and 'artillery-fired atomic projectiles are earmarked for deployment with the Marine Corps'.[45]

In order to bomb foreign territory, under normal operating conditions carrier-borne aircraft would have to operate within 800 km of the target, preferably much closer, although the risk of being intercepted or shot down increases as the aircraft approaches shore or the target. Accordingly, carrier air wings include dozens of sophisticated fighter aircraft which can escort and protect attack planes, and carrier battle groups are escorted by ships that have considerable anti-air warfare capabilities.

But in 1984 the navy began deploying a new generation of long-range weapons that will radically alter its ability to attack Soviet land targets: Tomahawk SLCMs. These new weapons are the key to the navy's expanded power projection mission. They will provide a new capability to some 200 naval vessels to launch attacks against land targets from greater distances than carriers can, and with greater chance of succeeding, thus increasing by more than an order of magnitude the navy's capability to launch such attacks. The most important characteristics of the SLCMs follow.

The sea-launched cruise missile is the most versatile and flexible weapon system in the US arsenal—conventional and nuclear. It serves strategic, theatre and tactical roles and will be the mainstay of the US 'strategic reserve' force, the nuclear weapons that would be held back in a nuclear war so that 'the United States would, in any post-nuclear exchange environment, retain a measure of coercive power'.[46] SLCMs can be installed on and fired from ships or submarines, given the proper launching equipment. The navy plans to install Tomahawks on two classes of attack submarine—Sturgeon (SSN-637) and Los Angeles (SSN-688)—and on six classes of surface ship—four recommissioned Iowa (BB-61) Class battleships, Spruance (DD-963) and Arleigh Burke (DDG-51) Class destroyers, Long Beach (CGN-9), Virginia (CG-38) and Ticonderoga (CG-47) Class cruisers (see table 28).[47] Thus, according to the head of the US cruise missile programme, the SLCM 'will allow virtually all navy combatants, not just the carrier battle groups, to go on the offensive whenever necessary and from any corner of the globe'.[48] The navy plans to build 3994 operational SLCMs, 758 of which will be nuclear-armed for land attack, 2643 will be conventionally armed for land attack and 593 will be anti-ship missiles with conventional warheads (see table 29). The nuclear land-attack variant has a range of 2500 kilometres (see table 30).

Since nuclear SLCMs will have more than twice the range of aircraft from carriers, they will augment the carriers in land-attack missions. According to the navy, SLCMs will be assigned to targets that aircraft carriers cannot strike, including 'targets deep inside enemy territory, currently outside the combat radius of tactical aircraft, point targets of extreme hardness, previously unable to be attacked with a high kill probability, and targets close to the FEBA [forward edge of battle area] that are so heavily defended as to cause excessively high levels of aircraft attrition'.[49] One navy official told the US Congress that the deployment of SLCMs assures that 'Soviet firepower cannot concentrate on the carrier alone' and provides 'an increase in the range of escalation control options available to the nation [US] without resort to central strategic systems'.[50] The navy has also stressed that Tomahawk SLCMs 'will increase the number of Warsaw Pact targets that are put at risk'.[51]

Table 28. US Tomahawk SLCM carriers, 1988[a] and 1995

Current number (1988)	Class	Number of vessels planned—1995	Number per vessel (nominal)
Submarines			
29	Los Angeles (SSN-688)	68	8 /12
37	Sturgeon (SSN-637)	39[b]	8/12
Surface ships			
3	Iowa (BB-61)	4	32
9 (4)[c]	Ticonderoga (CG-47)	22	26
4	Virginia (CG-38	4	8
1	Long Beach (CGN-9)	1	8
31	Spruance (DD-963)	31	45
0	Arleigh Burke (DDG-51)	29	28
Total		*198*	

[a] As of January 1988 there were 17 surface ships and 31 submarines equipped and certified to launch Tomahawk SLCMs.

[b] Includes one Narwhal Class and one Lipscomb Class submarine.

[c] The first five Ticonderoga Class cruisers (CG-47—CG-51) will not have the VLS nor Tomahawk SLCMs.

Sources: See table 12.

Sea control.   The US Navy maintains a large arsenal of nuclear weapons for sea control tasks, primarily for ASW (more than 1700 warheads) and AAW (some 300 warheads). Although the United States does not deploy nuclear weapons exclusively for anti-surface warfare, the JCS report that carrier-based nuclear-armed aircraft 'continue to provide the United States with a flexible nuclear land attack and antiship capability'.[52]

ASW.   ASW provides the best example of the importance of nuclear weapons for US naval warfare. The US Navy guide to nuclear warfare states:

One of the major contributions of nuclear weapons to the science of warfare is in the realm of ASW. Modern high-performance submarines pose an increasingly difficult target to attack successfully. Nuclear ASW weapons, with their greatly increased kill radius, provide an effective means to cope with this threat.[53]

Table 29. SLCM programme plan—1995

	TLAM/N	TLAM/C[a]	TASM[a]	Total
Submarines	270	838	293	*1401*
Surface ships	488	1805	300	*2593*
Total	*758*	*2643*	*593*	*3994*

[a] TLAM/N = Tomahawk Land Attack Missile/Nuclear;
TLAM/C = Tomahawk Land Attack Missile/Conventional;
TASM = Tomahawk Anti-Ship Missile.

Sources: See table 12.

Table 30. US Tomahawk nuclear SLCM—1988

Type	Number deployed	First year deployed	Range (km)	Warhead x yield	Warheads deployed
TLAM/N[a]	150	1984	2500	1 x 5-150 kt	150

[a] TLAM/N = Tomahawk Land Attack Missile/Nuclear.

Sources: See table 12.

There are some 1760 ASW nuclear warheads in the US arsenal, including 900 depth bombs for ASW aircraft and roughly 860 warheads for missiles launched by surface ships and submarines.[54] Although the navy has conventional torpedoes for ASW, nuclear weapons are kept for situations when conventional ones cannot guarantee the destruction of an enemy submarine. According to the US Navy: '...to prevent the possibility that improvements in Soviet systems could negate, at some point, the capabilities of our conventional ASW weapons, we must have nuclear ASW weapons.'[55]

The fact that the USA has five nuclear ASW weapons for every Soviet submarine (not just the modern SSBNs) demonstrates that the United States has a large capacity to use nuclear weapons against those submarines in war. US contingency plans to deploy hundreds of nuclear depth bombs to foreign coastal bases in a crisis or war further demonstrate the important role of nuclear weapons for ASW.[56] If the stated navy wartime goal of destroying Soviet submarines, including SSBNs, proves unfeasible with conventional weapons, the navy has its nuclear 'back-up' ready.

There are three types of nuclear ASW weapon in the US arsenal, one for each type of naval vessel: ship-launched *anti-submarine rock*ets (ASROCs) that can carry a nuclear depth charge, SUBROCs that carry a nuclear depth charge, and B-57 depth bombs for land- and sea-based ASW aircraft (see table 31). ASROC, an unguided dual-capable short-range rocket, is the most widely deployed nuclear weapon system among surface ships. It is aboard almost all major surface combatants, including cruisers, destroyers and frigates, nearly 160 ships in all. There are 575 of the W44 nuclear warheads deployed for ASROC, which was first operational in 1961. The navy plans to introduce a new Vertical Launch ASROC (VLA) to replace the current system. Although the navy wanted VLA to be nuclear-capable, it now appears that the missile will be conventional only.

The 285 SUBROC missiles are capable of being deployed on five classes of attack submarine: Los Angeles (SSN-688), Lipscomb (SSN-685), Narwhal (SSN-671), Sturgeon (SSN-637) and Permit (SSN-594). However, since there are only one each of the Lipscomb and Narwhal Classes, the bulk of SUBROC deployments are aboard the other three classes, including the first 12 Los Angeles Class submarines, but primarily in Sturgeon and Permit submarines.[57] SUBROC is designed to be fired from standard 21-inch (533-mm) torpedo tubes, then to break through the sea surface, fly through the air on its rocket booster and, at a calculated distance, drop back into the water to release its nuclear depth charge, which detonates at a predetermined depth. Having first been deployed in 1965, the SUBROC began being phased out of service in the mid-1980s and is scheduled to be replaced by an ASW Stand-off Weapon beginning in the 1990s. As with all

Table 31. US nuclear ASW weapons—1988

Weapon	First year deployed	Range (km)	Warhead x yield	Warheads deployed	Platforms
ASROC	1961	1-10	1 x 5-10 kt	574	*Cruisers:* Leahy, Belknap, Long Beach, Bainbridge, Truxtun, California, Virginia, Ticonderoga (first 5); *Destroyers:* Spruance, Adams, Farragut, Kidd; *Frigates:* Bronstein, Garcia, Knox, Glover, Brooke
SUBROC	1965	60	1 x 5-10 kt	285	Los Angeles, Sturgeon, Permit, Narwhal, Lipscomb
B57 depth bombs[a]	1963	—	1 x <20 kt	897	P-3B/C, S-3A/B, SH-3D/H

[a] B57 nuclear depth bombs are stored on land for P-3 aircraft, and aboard aircraft carriers for S-3 and SH-3 aircraft.

Sources: See table 12.

other US nuclear ASW weapons, SUBROC could conceivably also be used for anti-ship or land-attack missions.

B57 nuclear depth bombs are the most numerous type of ASW weapon in the US arsenal, with 900 deployed. These bombs are deployed at land bases for P-3 maritime patrol aircraft and aboard aircraft carriers for S-3A aircraft and SH-3 helicopters deployed at sea. The navy will purchase new helicopters, SH-60F models, to replace SH-3s, and will modernize the S-3 force beginning in the late 1980s. Some of the US depth bombs are set aside for use by British, Italian and Dutch ASW aircraft. There are over 400 P-3 Orion aircraft in the navy inventory, divided among 24 active and 13 reserve squadrons. These Orions rotate to numerous seaside bases around the world in peacetime, and plans have been drawn up to send them with their B57 nuclear depth bombs to even more foreign bases, some in non-nuclear or nuclear weapon-free countries, in a crisis or war.[58]

The US Navy has tried to develop new nuclear warheads for a new 'series' of ASW weapons to augment and eventually to replace those currently in the stockpile. These efforts have run into difficulty in the US Congress, primarily because the navy has provided weak justifications for them, and it remains to be seen to what degree Congress will fund the navy's requested thorough nuclear modernization.[59]

AAW. Nuclear weapons have been part of the navy's anti-air warfare arsenal since the early 1950s, but only recently has it become apparent that the navy is renewing its interest in nuclear weapons for AAW. The currently deployed weapon system is the Terrier SAM deployed on 21 cruisers and 10 destroyers. There are 285 nuclear warheads stockpiled for the Terriers, although the missile and warhead are scheduled to be replaced with Standard SAMs by the mid-1990s.

The primary purpose of these weapons is to shoot down approaching enemy aircraft or incoming anti-ship missiles, 'especially those aboard Backfire and Badger bombers'.[60] Since Backfire, Badger and other Soviet naval bombers carry nuclear ASCMs, and new Soviet nuclear SLCMs pose an increasing danger to US surface forces, the premium on destroying air and missile forces is increasing. Defense Secretary Weinberger noted that 'because they are difficult to intercept, the missiles can best be countered by detecting and engaging the aircraft and vessels that carry them'.[61] The navy has been trying to get congressional funding to produce a new nuclear warhead—the W81—that has already been designed for the Standard Missile. Because of its numerous failures to convince the US Congress of the merits of the nuclear version of the Standard Missile—SM-2 (N)—the US Navy appears to have given up the effort, at least temporarily. The navy has also studied a nuclear warhead for the Phoenix air-to-air missile (AAM), although the Phoenix warhead plan appears to have been shelved.

Although the navy has had difficulty convincing Congress to pay for a whole new generation of non-strategic nuclear weapons, it has procured other systems which have increased its ability to use nuclear weapons at sea. The most important such system is the Vertical Launch System (VLS), which will be installed on most new classes of combat ships and submarines. VLS is a modular missile launch system that permits a vessel to carry a large and diverse mixture of missiles for several purposes. It will be able to fire Tomahawk SLCMs, Standard Missiles, Harpoon ASCMs, a new Vertical Launch ASROC, the ASW Standoff Weapon now in development and other future missiles. Most of these were designed to be nuclear or nuclear-capable systems, although some plans have changed. Compared with previous missile launchers, VLS will enable ships and submarines to carry a wider variety of missiles and, in some cases, many more.[62] It will provide for greater flexibility, quicker response time and greater survivability than its predecessors. Furthermore, with VLS all missiles are available for immediate launch in contrast to previous systems that required a pause before missiles could be loaded onto the few launch rails available. A 12-missile VLS, called the Capsule Launch System (CLS), mounted in the bow of new submarines will permit those submarines to carry 12 Tomahawk or Harpoon SLCMs without taking up limited weapon storage space inside the submarine. This will allow for a larger load of weapons, including torpedoes, SUBROCs and Tomahawks. Since VLS will carry both conventional and nuclear systems and will be installed below the decks of ships and submarines, it will make any attempt at arms control verification or determining nuclear capability even more difficult than today.

British non-strategic naval nuclear forces

The United Kingdom maintains an estimated 168 nuclear weapons for naval warfare, 134 depth bombs for ASW and 34 gravity bombs for land-attack or for attacks against surface ships (see table 32). Three Invincible Class aircraft carriers, 12 destroyers and 8 frigates are equipped to use these nuclear systems, a substantial portion of the fleet. Four types of aircraft are in service with these nuclear bombs, and another is certified to use US nuclear depth bombs.

Table 32.   British and French non-strategic naval nuclear forces—1988

Type/Model	Number deployed	First year deployed	Nuclear weapons	Warheads deployed	Platform
UK					
Strike aircraft[a]					
Sea Harrier FRS.1	34	1980	1 x bomb	34	3 Invincible Class aircraft carriers
ASW helicopters					
Sea King HAS.5	56	1976	1 x depth bomb	56	Invincible Class, Type 22 frigates
Lynx HAS.2/3	78	1976	1 x depth bomb	78	Type 42 destroyers, Type 22 frigates
Total	*168*			*168*	
France					
Strike Aircraft					
Super Etendard	36	1978	1 x bomb, or ASMP missile[b]	36	2 Clemenceau Class aircraft carriers

[a]The British Royal Air Force also operates some 25 Buccaneer S.2B and 31 Nimrod MR.2 nuclear-capable aircraft that have anti-ship and anti-submarine warfare duties, respectively. The USA stockpiles nuclear depth bombs for the Nimrod aircraft.

[b] From 1988, the Super Etendard will carry the Air-Sol-Moyenne-Portée (ASMP) nuclear-armed air-to-surface missile, instead of a gravity bomb.

Sources: See table 12.

Power projection/land attack. Most of the UK's nuclear power projection might resides in the strategic submarine fleet. However, Britain has three aircraft carriers which can accommodate nuclear-capable. Sea Harrier FRS.1 attack aircraft. There is usually one squadron of 5-8 Sea Harriers aboard each aircraft carrier. Those aircraft not on the carriers are based on land, but are available for carrier duty. The

Sea Harriers can carry the British WE-177 nuclear gravity bomb, of which there are an estimated 50 for land attacks or for anti-ship attacks.

Sea control. Most of Britain's non-strategic naval nuclear capability is in its ASW forces, although there is a land-based maritime strike capability. The land-based Sea Harriers and 25 Buccaneer bombers are available for nuclear ASUW tasks, primarily to attack adversary ships with WE-177 nuclear gravity bombs. For ASW the UK has nearly 140 sea- and land-based helicopters and 31 land-based Nimrod maritime patrol aircraft. There are 78 Lynx HAS.2/3 and 56 Sea King HAS.5 ASW helicopters operating from 23 surface ships. Sea Kings are aboard the three aircraft carriers and aboard Type 22 frigates. The 12 Type 42 destroyers can carry Lynx helicopters, as can the frigates. Each helicopter can carry one British nuclear depth bomb, about which little is publicly known but which is thought to be a low-yield version of the Royal Air Force tactical bomb.[63] The 31 Nimrod ASW aircraft are certified to use US B57 nuclear depth bombs stored for them in England.

French non-strategic naval nuclear forces

France, even more than Britain, puts most of its naval nuclear forces in its ballistic missile submarines. The exception to this rule is that France operates two aircraft carriers—the *Clemenceau* and the *Foch*—for which Super Etendard attack aircraft have been deployed for land-attack and anti-ship purposes since 1978. Of some 56 Super Etendards in the French Navy, 36 are assigned to the carriers and the rest are available for reserve duty from land bases. Each of the Super Etendards can carry one nuclear gravity bomb, either the ANT-52 or possibly a lower-yield alternative,[64] or one nuclear air-to-surface missile (see table 32). Both carriers are homeported at Toulon in the Mediterranean Sea. One of the carriers usually operates in the Mediterranean, or in either the Atlantic or the Indian Ocean/Persian Gulf region.

France plans to replace the ANT-52 gravity bombs for Super Etendards with its new ASMP (Air-Sol-Moyenne-Portée) air-to-surface missile (ASM) beginning in 1988. The ASMP has a yield of 300 kt and a range of up to 250 km, thereby increasing French carrier-based land-attack capability considerably. Super Etendards started being modified to carry the ASMP in 1984, with 53 aircraft planned for the final pro-gramme. France has announced plans to replace its two current aircraft carriers with new nuclear-powered carriers. The keel of the first carrier, to be named *Richelieu*, was laid in 1986, and it is scheduled to join the fleet by 1997. If France proceeds as planned, the order to replace the other carrier is expected to be placed about 1990.

V. Arms control and security impact

Naval forces with nuclear weapons pose special problems and risks for conflict and arms control alike. The thousands of naval nuclear weapons described in the preceding sections require special attention in any arms control or security-building effort. Since naval non-strategic nuclear weapons have received so little attention in the past, there has been almost no study of their impact for arms control or security, particularly with respect to issues of their influence on the probability of conflict and the risks of their use and escalation.[65]

Assessing the security impact of these weapons is necessarily a somewhat speculative venture as it depends on numerous unprovable assumptions and predictions of behaviour under unpredictable conditions. However, it is clear that there are extraordinary dangers and risks involved, and that arms control issues and possibilities need to be raised and examined critically. These topics will be covered here briefly, as much to present the issues and raise questions that need to be subjected to a rigorous debate as to suggest possible approaches for the future.

This section begins with a brief survey of the general conditions that influence discussions of naval nuclear weapons and is followed by an assessment of their impact on security and arms control, respectively.

The first important fact to consider is that naval forces operate in international waters without much regulation as these waters are largely beyond any form of national jurisdiction. Free passage on the high seas, freedom of navigation, the right of innocent passage and similar concepts have not only become enshrined in international law, they have become the paramount principles of navies world-wide. Consequently, naval forces have much greater freedom of action than their land or air force counterparts, and navies are disposed to guarding that freedom above almost everything else.

Concerning nuclear weapons, as with all other naval prerogatives, the superpower navies appear to want to preserve all their options and, especially with the US Navy, not to permit each other or any other power to impinge upon their freedom of action on the seas. Part of this effort employs secrecy, as seen in the practice of nuclear navies neither confirming nor denying the presence of nuclear weapons aboard their vessels.

Superpower secrecy surrounding naval nuclear weapon matters is more extensive, and more counterproductive, than with their land or air forces. Given the relatively small number of combat vessels available (ships, submarines and aircraft), one can make reasonable and militarily prudent assumptions about the operational nuclear practices of the nuclear navies, thus negating the military effect of secrecy. (In a war both superpowers would presumably attack any enemy naval vessel, regardless of its armament.) The 'neither confirm nor deny' practice guarantees that port visits by any nuclear-capable (and even many non-nuclear-capable) ship(s) will be assumed to be nuclear-armed visits, and will create public opposition and political discord. This occurs even within the NATO alliance, as the Danish election of May 1988 demonstrated. Furthermore, there is almost no public discussion of nuclear matters within the navies, including the most basic information as to why nuclear weapons are considered useful or necessary, or what alternatives to non-strategic nuclear weapons might exist .

Contradictions and inconsistencies abound in the limited discussion of the issue within the US Navy, which is virtually the only navy that discusses nuclear weapon issues in public. Thus, as a starting point, one works with a paucity of information, much of it basic to an informed debate. Some previous US-Soviet arms control negotiations have resulted in greatly improved explanation and mutual understanding of both nation's policies and programmes, as well as proscriptions for future programmes. Since the US and Soviet Navies appear uncertain about each other's, and possibly their own, non-strategic nuclear weapons, this result might be one goal for any discussion of naval nuclear weapons.

Danger of nuclear war at sea

It is possible, some say likely, that nuclear war might start at sea. Given the widespread deployment of nuclear weapons with the US and Soviet Navies and their increasing capacity to use these weapons, the possibility needs to be examined carefully. Recent developments in weapons and technology, strategy, and operating procedures and exercises suggest that there is an increasing likelihood of nuclear war starting at sea in the course of a US-Soviet war and rapidly escalating to a global nuclear war.[66] The US Navy argues the opposite case while pursuing contradictory policies and forces. In order to permit a full debate, it is necessary to present the arguments on this topic.

There are numerous reasons why nuclear weapons might be used at sea in a crisis or war between the USA and the USSR. The most prominent are briefly presented below.

• In naval warfare generally, and in any superpower naval battle particularly, the premium on shooting first (what Admiral Gorshkov called the 'struggle for the first salvo') may be dangerously, if not unbearably, high. Consequently, navies are often trying to get the best tactical positioning at sea to minimize the effects and temptation of adversary pre-emption, or to be in position to shoot first. Secretary of Defense Weinberger made this point bluntly in his FY 1988 annual report: 'Naval modernization programs emphasize the development of weapons and tactics that allow our forces—once hostilities have been initiated—to strike first, from extended ranges.'[67]

This problem appears most acute with the possibility of Soviet first nuclear use and US retaliation, since the USSR does not have the conventional firepower for a decisive first salvo attack and may rely on nuclear weapons to stop an overwhelming naval attack from the USA. This set of assumptions is behind the US policy on escalation of Soviet nuclear first use at sea: to threaten nuclear retaliation against land targets with SLCMs or other land-attack systems to dissuade the Soviet Union from going nuclear first, or at all. This policy raises questions about credibility, escalation and the idea of a 'limited' use of nuclear weapons at sea, none of which the navy addresses satisfactorily.

• There are numerous reasons postulated as to why nuclear weapons could be used at sea more readily than on land. It is possible that political or military leaders could believe that the use of nuclear weapons at sea could be contained or limited to the sea, and not escalate to use on land. Since nuclear attacks *at sea* presumably would not involve attacks on national territory, or directly against civilian populations, the risk of escalation is often considered lower than with attacks on land. As stated in the US Navy guide to nuclear war operations, 'in a limited war at sea resulting from attempts to hinder or sever lines of communication, both parties to the conflict might be reluctant to extend the war to the land or use nuclear weapons except at sea'.[68]

This notion of a reduced risk of further escalation in response to nuclear attacks at sea underlies the US policy to threaten nuclear attacks against the USSR if it initiates nuclear attacks against the US Navy. This fact alone shows that naval nuclear weapons are thought of differently than weapons on land. But it also shows that the risk of escalation is not just theoretical; it is a national policy option for at least the USA. Both superpower navies are increasing their capabilities to attack land targets with nuclear weapons.

Of course, one must not forget that naval warfare would only be part of a larger conflict involving land and air forces. Thus, the stakes would automatically be higher in any US-Soviet naval confrontation than just an isolated incident at sea. Furthermore, naval warfare itself would *not* be confined to the sea. It would invariably spread to the many naval targets ashore, including ports, airfields, and naval command and control facilities, among others.

If the NATO flexible response option of responding to conventional attacks with nuclear weapons is taken seriously, it is difficult to see why the USSR would not consider using nuclear weapons against US nuclear-armed naval forces, particularly against the carriers and cruise-missile-carrying vessels that the US Navy says are high-priority targets for the USSR. Since the US Navy has the conventional and nuclear capability to threaten the destruction of the Soviet Navy, its ballistic missile submarines and land targets across the USSR, the Soviet leadership would probably contemplate using whatever means necessary, including nuclear weapons, to defend against these forces if attacked. US naval non-strategic nuclear weapons represent roughly as much nuclear firepower as is contained in NATO's nuclear arsenal, both of which the USSR understands are devastating sources of potential destruction.

• Command and control of naval nuclear weapons is a thorny subject. Since only national political authorities are assumed to be able to authorize the use of naval nuclear weapons, several considerations arise. First is the question of how, when and under what circumstances political authorities would permit the use of naval nuclear weapons. Unlike most other US nuclear weapons, naval nuclear weapons are not equipped with physical control devices, known as permissive action links (PALs). These electromechanical devices are intended to prevent the accidental or unauthorized use of nuclear weapons by requiring a special code to be transmitted to the firing unit in order to arm the weapon. The lack of PALs is partly explained by the potential difficulty of assuring direct communications between the so-called 'National Command Authorities' and naval vessels in wartime, particularly submarines, to transmit the necessary codes. But it is also partly due to navy opposition to the physical and political controls that are required for other US nuclear weapons.

It could, therefore, be difficult either to prevent their unauthorized use or to grant permission quickly to naval forces which find themselves under attack. In 1983 Admiral W. Holland, then Director of Strategic and Theatre Nuclear Warfare for the US Navy, testified to the US Congress that the problem of political control and release authority for nuclear weapons at sea was unsolved: 'We have not come to grips with that part of the problem.'69 Although it is considered highly unlikely that US or Soviet political leaders would give advance nuclear authorization to naval forces,70 in a crisis the US Navy may feel pressured to operate as though they had pre-delegated authorization. This calls into question the credibility of entire classes of nuclear weapons that may be unusable unless naval commanders use them without authorization in a war, which raises serious questions about the effectiveness of political control over nuclear forces at sea. The current situation without PALs may amount to little more than an implicit form of pre-delegated nuclear authorization.

This is not to say that it is assumed that either political or military authorities take lightly the issue of using nuclear weapons (crossing the nuclear threshold). Nevertheless, examples of modern crisis and combat have shown before that political control of naval forces was less than complete.71 It is unclear what conditions or actions would transpire in a major war between the two superpowers, but nuclear stockpiles and practices are most discouraging. The very posturing and activities of the two nuclear superpowers in a crisis could run out of control,72 and both sides are planning for a final war. Thus, despite the assumption that nuclear weapons will never be used—even in a US-Soviet war—it is more than possible. The possibility need not be large in peacetime to pose a catastrophic and unacceptable risk. And what appears improbable in peacetime may become inevitable in a war.

• It is often noted that naval forces, particularly submarines, are becoming more difficult to cripple or destroy with conventional weapons, at least without using an inordinate quantity of conventional ammunition. There may, therefore, be incentives to use nuclear weapons to assure that attacks succeed and that targets are destroyed. As Secretary of Defense Weinberger stated in his annual report for FY 1987: 'In addition to deterring Soviet first use of similar nuclear weapons at sea, US nuclear antiair and antisubmarine weapons provide unique capabilities that serve as a backup for our conventional systems.'[73] In other words, if conventional weapons cannot guarantee the destruction of enemy forces, we have nuclear weapons available—not only for retaliation.

There is widespread concern within Western naval circles that conventional ASW weapons may not be able to sink modern Soviet submarines. (It is not clear whether this stems from the poor historical record of torpedoes in warfare, from unreasonably high damage requirements for ASW, or from worries created by the lack of opportunity to test the weapons against their intended targets.) The result is that the US Navy has acquired over 1700 nuclear ASW weapons—in case the conventional ones do not work. Given the fact that the Soviet Navy also has many nuclear ASW weapons, including nuclear torpedoes, it presumably has similar concerns about conventional ASW. This tacit acknowledgement that both superpowers may feel it necessary to use nuclear weapons for ASW puts an ominous twist on the notion of conventional naval warfare.

As a result of increasing superpower naval nuclear capabilities, US and Soviet naval vessels have undergone nuclear-hardening programmes in recent years to reduce the effects of nuclear attacks. Admiral Powell Carter, then director of the US Navy's nuclear warfare division, told the US Congress in 1981: 'We are working hard on improving ship survivability. We have revamped the training command in order to teach our people to think nuclear. We are extending to where all of our exercises are into a nuclear phase.'[74]

Risks of escalation

One of the most contentious but least resolvable issues concerning naval nuclear weapons is that of escalation. The basic question concerns the probability and possibility of some nation initiating the use of nuclear weapons at sea, and the consequent reactions. On one level it is an issue fraught with subjective predispositions and assumptions about adversary incentives and psychology in war. On another level it is a clear-cut issue: *any* war between the superpowers carries tremendous risk that nuclear weapons will be used and the war will escalate into a global nuclear war; that is the very threat that has been assumed to keep peace since World War II.

The issue of escalation is important for the first level of thinking, where most policy-makers and military officials dwell, but not for the second. The USA and the USSR base numerous decisions, policies, strategies, tactics and weapon choices partly on their assumptions about escalation, which are prone to being mistaken.

Many facets of this problem simply have not been considered.[75] The conclusions drawn by the few navy professionals who have studied the issue, as they admit, could well be wrong, as have been previous predictions of events in crisis and war.[76] It is not clear what Soviet thinking is on the subject, although it seems to have changed considerably since the 1960s away from the conclusion that any use of nuclear weapons would inevitably lead to immediate global nuclear war.[77] Nevertheless, the Soviet Navy has steadily increased its nuclear capabilities over 30 years and shows no sign of decreasing its interest in having a vast array of nuclear weapons. Even if one does not know exactly what the Soviet leadership and Navy think or plan, one must ask why the Soviet Navy has acquired such a large arsenal of nuclear weapons and with it a great capacity for escalation. These features certainly worry the USA. US perspectives are discussed below.

Discussions of escalation often differentiate between the first use of nuclear weapons at sea, or after they have been used first on land. It is considered highly unlikely that there would be any disincentive to using nuclear weapons at sea once they have been used on land. However, the US Navy argues publicly that Soviet leaders have no incentive to use nuclear weapons at sea and are so determined to keep any conflict non-nuclear that they simply will not permit the Soviet Navy to do so.[78] Similarly, the US Navy dismisses the risk of nuclear war at sea beginning after nuclear attacks against land targets, since the Soviet Union is too prudent to start using nuclear weapons on land. This 'conventional' wisdom entirely excludes the possibility that NATO would use nuclear weapons first on land in Europe, as is its declared policy option. Seemingly little thought has been given to this aspect of nuclear escalation at sea, despite US officials acknowledging plans for firing nuclear warning shots in a European war.[79]

A brief discussion of the current official thinking about naval nuclear escalation will demonstrate the inconsistent and contradictory nature of discourse.

The US maritime strategy seeks to provide 'war termination leverage' against the USSR, which is a euphemistic way of saying one poses such a strong threat to the Soviet Union that in a war it must choose between defeat and peace on US/NATO terms. Any such threat would have to be severe, but presumably not sufficiently provocative to result in a pre-emptive Soviet nuclear strike.

One major feature of the US strategy's purported leverage is the threat of sinking Soviet SSBNs, traditionally regarded as the least vulnerable and therefore the most 'stabilizing' nuclear weapon systems. US maritime strategy advocates claim that the Soviet SSBN force is important enough to Soviet leaders as a 'reserve force' that its attrition or loss would force the USSR to negotiate a settlement, but would not draw a nuclear response. According to former Chief of Naval Operations Admiral James Watkins:

The Soviets place great weight on the nuclear correlation of forces, even during the time before nuclear weapons have been used. Maritime forces can influence that nuclear correlation, both by destroying Soviet ballistic missile submarines and by improving our own nuclear posture, through deployment of carriers and Tomahawk platforms around the periphery of the Soviet Union. Some argue that such steps will lead to immediate escalation, but escalation solely as a result of actions at sea seems improbable, given the Soviet land orientation. Escalation in response to maritime pressure would serve no useful purpose for the Soviets since their [nuclear] reserve forces would be degraded and the United States retaliatory posture would be enhanced.[80]

Nevertheless, should the Soviet leadership contemplate using nuclear weapons against the US Navy in the hope of confining their use to sea, the USA has adopted a policy of threatening nuclear retaliation against Soviet land targets in response to Soviet first nuclear use at sea. According to various reports, the secret US Defense Guidance Document for 1984-1988 states: 'It will be US policy that a nuclear war beginning with Soviet nuclear attacks at sea will not necessarily remain limited to the sea... The prospect of losing their fleet to US naval theater forces may not be sufficient to deter the Soviets from initiating a nuclear campaign at sea.'[81]

This clearly demonstrates two facts that belie the 'conventional' wisdom argument. First, it shows the US concern for Soviet incentives and capabilities to use nuclear weapons at sea. If the prospect of losing their navy to US naval nuclear forces is not enough to dissuade the USSR from starting a nuclear war at sea, then it must have some compelling incentives for doing so. Second, any actions the US Navy takes that increase Soviet incentives for using nuclear weapons, such as attacking Soviet SSBNS, will only exacerbate the problem and increase the danger. Furthermore, this policy means that the USA does not really believe that its naval nuclear weapons would necessarily deter the

USSR from using nuclear weapons first, thus undercutting any argument for the deterrent value of such US weapons.

The US defence community appears to agree that the primary purpose of the Soviet Navy in war would be to protect Soviet SSBNs and Soviet territory from US attack, and that these are high priorities in Soviet defence planning. In discussing Soviet naval war goals, Admiral Watkins wrote: 'Soviet doctrine gives a high priority to locating and destroying Western sea-based nuclear assets, including aircraft carriers, ballistic missile submarines, and Tomahawk-equipped plat- forms. The Soviets would particularly like to be able to destroy our ballistic missile submarines, but lack the antisubmarine warfare capability to implement such a mission.'[82]

If this is true, then the US Navy should not be too sanguine about its prediction that nuclear weapons would not be used. The idea that the USSR considers US nuclear-capable naval forces high-priority targets contradicts Watkins' non-escalation notion and suggests that nuclear weapons would be on the Soviet options list.

Although militarily the USSR is indeed dominated by land concerns and land forces officers, it is important to note the contradiction that this poses for the US Navy. If US Navy attempts at sinking the Soviet fleet, sinking its submarines and attacking land targets are significant enough to cause the Soviet Union to give up in a war, they are significant enough to warrant desperate measures, including using nuclear weapons. In other words, if the USSR perceives that its survival or existence as a state is threatened in a war, it would strongly consider using nuclear weapons, as would the USA or any other nuclear weapon state. This makes the land power argument moot and the prospect of such attacks most dangerous.

If, however, the land orientation argument is correct, and the USSR would not care about the destruction of its naval and SLBM forces, then the US maritime strategy is irrelevant to the outcome of a war and would neither hasten its termination nor prevent its occurrence in the first place.

Policies on naval nuclear weapons

The foregoing discussion examined only the issues of nuclear escalation as they apply to current superpower naval affairs. It did not treat other issues, such as, the credibility of such a strategy or the feasibility of implementing it. But it does bring us back to the first question concerning naval nuclear weapons: Why do the nuclear navies have them? As with all other nuclear weapon issues, the dearth of publicly available information prevents observers from examining this issue in sufficient detail.

A determined nuclear attack against naval forces would be both immensely destructive and difficult to defend against; only one warhead need slip past the defences to succeed. The basic justification for naval nuclear weapons is twofold. First, by possessing nuclear weapons one can deter an adversary from using them. This is the deterrence argument. Second, possessing nuclear weapons provides a navy with the option to use them in a crisis or war—whether it is to fire a nuclear warning shot, to assure the destruction of a given target, to destroy an adversary's naval forces in a pre-emptive attack, in retaliation for an adversary using nuclear weapons, or for some other war-fighting purpose. This is the war-fighting argument. (While these two arguments are markedly different, they are usually confused in the rare US Navy explanations of its non-strategic nuclear forces.)

Although it seems unlikely that either superpower navy would ever choose, or be permitted, to launch a massive nuclear first strike against the other, even the possibility of sudden nuclear attacks and their consequences induce the USA and the USSR to stockpile nuclear weapons for offensive and defensive purposes—both for deterring and fighting wars. The nuclear navies' perceived need for self-defence against such improbable nuclear attacks, and the desire to have a nuclear option for destroying their adversary, propel the 'requirements' for existing and new nuclear weapons, thus driving the arms race spiral. Using nuclear weapons to attack naval forces may offer a high probability of target destruction, but the likely minimum consequence may be the nuclear devastation of both navies. Escalation to general nuclear war could well follow.

The US Navy's claimed requirement or need for naval non-strategic nuclear weapons leaves important questions unanswered. US Navy policy on nuclear weapons contradicts its statements and declared strategy for war. On the one hand, its current strategy supposes that a prolonged, global conventional war can be fought and won against the Soviet Navy without resort to nuclear weapons.[83] Yet the US Navy also states that: 'It is not Navy policy to buy nuclear weapons automatically as replacements for systems being retired. We require a clear case for the utility of each weapon. Nuclear weapons should not serve as substitutes for conventional weapons where improved conventional weapons will suffice. We will procure only those nuclear weapons which provide a unique and substantial military capability.'[84] If this statement is true, it casts a different light on naval nuclear weapons, suggesting that the US Navy views them as necessary for fighting, not just deterring war. Either nuclear weapons are considered necessary for fighting war or not. If not, they may be militarily undesirable because they are neither credible nor usable against a heavily armed nuclear navy and because their use could likely lead to rapid escalation and to general nuclear war. The US Navy does not address or resolve this contradiction.

Arms control issues

Both superpowers have officially pledged themselves to the goal of eliminating all nuclear weapons. In spite of this fact, neither seems to have done any serious work on the question of eliminating naval nuclear weapons. It is therefore important to begin thinking about the topic seriously.

There are numerous reasons why naval officers and planners could be interested in reducing or even eliminating non-strategic nuclear weapons, basically because it would serve their naval and national interests, but also because nuclear weapons require special handling and procedures that complicate every aspect of naval operations.

If non-strategic naval nuclear weapons were greatly reduced or eliminated, it could have far-reaching and positive effects. For the USA, the most important point is that the navy would not only retain its strong margin of advantage over the Soviet Navy, but also its ability to carry out its missions would be enhanced. The only way that the Soviet Navy could destroy the US Navy is with nuclear weapons; without such a capacity the Soviet Navy poses a much smaller threat to its superior rival. If the USSR retains its large naval nuclear arsenal, then all US naval advantages—which can only apply to conventional forces—are put at great risk. For the USSR, the most important point is that it would reduce the considerable nuclear threat to its territory and to its navy from the US Navy, a security enhancement which is of paramount interest.

Both nations (and their navies) could see other advantages to having few or no non-strategic naval nuclear weapons:

• There would be less risk of escalation of any naval confrontation to nuclear war.

• There would be less risk of being a nuclear target and of a miscalculation that one side is preparing to use nuclear weapons.

• There would be less pressure to prepare for or respond quickly to a massive 'first salvo' nuclear attack, thus reducing nuclear crisis pressures.

• And, there would be no need to stockpile nuclear weapons throughout the fleets to deter the use of similar adversary systems.

A ship operating without nuclear weapons aboard might be preferable to a commanding officer (CO) and crew for several reasons. It would give the CO more flexibility and freedom of operation and decision in peacetime, crisis and war, since there would be no need to be restricted by or to consider the question or procedures of using nuclear weapons. There would be fewer safety risks aboard vessels from handling, transporting and maintaining nuclear weapons, which would mean less of the necessary but time-consuming and cumbersome paperwork and bureaucracy that come with nuclear weapons. There would be fewer problems with command, control and communications to and from higher military and political authorities. There would be no political problems with port calls to nations that do not permit nuclear weapons in their territorial waters or ports. There would be more space available for non-nuclear systems and ammunition, which is the only kind a CO can be sure will be usable in a conflict.

These features and more might logically appeal to naval professionals as good reasons to consider reducing or eliminating the nuclear weapons in their supposedly conventional navies. However, there appears to be a tendency for navies to want to keep nuclear weapons in the fleet, perhaps because of some perceived prestige of having a nuclear capability and mission, or perhaps just because of habit. But it is clear that there is no public discussion of these issues by the navy; concerning nuclear weapons, the navy is indeed the silent service.

As for the traditional arms control arguments, the most difficult issue tends to be verification, although there has not been sufficient study of this problem, and it is possible that predominant political and naval attitudes may be more serious problems. Resolving verification issues will depend both on the goal to be achieved and on the degree of commitment to that goal. Given the current advances in verification cooperation between the USA and the USSR, on chemical weapons, at the Stockholm Conference, in the INF Treaty, and at the START negotiations, one can at least discuss new possibilities, however difficult. If the Soviet leadership wants its proposals for nuclear disarmament to be considered seriously, it is, at a minimum, incumbent upon the USSR to present the necessary and detailed verification concepts and measures.

The one category of naval non-strategic nuclear weapons which logically should be included in existing US-Soviet arms control deliberations are SLCMs. Although they clearly have the potential to be used like strategic weapons, SLCMs were not included in any of the relevant negotiations (INF or START) until late 1987. Previous considerations of SLCMS, for example at SALT II, ended in the conclusion that verification problems alone were insurmountable and thus not worth trying to solve. The primary negotiating hurdles concern the fact that there are many varieties of SLCMs with different missions and ranges, and that only a portion of them are nuclear or nuclear-capable. Since less than one-quarter of the planned Tomahawks will be nuclear-armed, it complicates any attempt to control, limit or eliminate them. Soviet SLCMs are even more varied and widespread.

Until the US-Soviet summit meeting of 7-10 December 1987, there was no progress visible on the issue of controlling nuclear SLCMs. But it was apparent to both nations, particularly at Soviet insistence, that a START agreement could not completely overlook long-range nuclear SLCMs capable of attacking land targets on their respective territories. The INF Treaty signed at the summit bans ground-launched cruise missiles, and the START negotiations include air-launched versions. Only SLCMs remained outside the arms control process. So the two governments committed themselves for the first time to pursue SLCM limitations. According to the joint summit statement of 10 December 1987:[85]

The sides shall find a mutually acceptable solution to the question of limiting the deployment of long-range, nuclear-armed SLCMs. ... The sides committed themselves to establishing ceilings on such missiles, and to seek mutually acceptable and effective methods of verification of such limitations, which could include the employment of National Technical Means, cooperative measures, and on-site inspection.

Both nations also agreed that any SLCM limitations would not be included within the agreed START numerical limits, but would be considered within the START process and negotiations. The most difficult problem appears to be verification. The USSR made proposals at the summit for verifying SLCM limits, but the USA expressed scepticism about their feasibility. Part of the problem depends on what ultimate solution the two sides attempt to reach; permitting several hundred nuclear SLCMs would be harder to verify than a ban on all such missiles.

Various proposals and ideas have been discussed, and the two nations have agreed to study the issue and to consider joint verification experiments. One far-reaching possibility was raised by the senior US arms control adviser, Paul Nitze, during US deliberations: eliminating all naval non-strategic nuclear weapons.[86] Generally speaking, such an outright ban could make verification simpler, as it did in the INF Treaty. Although the idea met with some strong opposition, the fact that Nitze raised it is an indication that the discussion has opened to ideas that were never raised before. Clearly, the prospects for SLCM limitations have moved far beyond the traditional unwillingness to consider such controls seriously. Still, many difficulties and opportunities for failure remain.

No other non-strategic nuclear weapons are considered in other negotiations. These weapons are developed and deployed without any serious arms control impact analysis or concern, including their necessity, verifiabililty, suitability for crises, C^3 problems, and so forth. This creates difficulties for any subsequent efforts at arms control or disarmament. Two developments illustrate the point.

Dual-capable weapon systems, those that can use either nuclear or non-nuclear warheads, are considered important and efficient by the superpower navies because only one type of launcher is needed, thus freeing valuable and limited space for ammunition and other stores aboard ships and submarines. Vertical launching systems are the most recent refinement of the dual-capable principle. They combine dual capability with the ability to store and launch multiple missile types in rapid sequence, thus eliminating the need for a separate storage magazine, while remaining below the ship's deck. Both types of system are efficient, but reflect a lack of concern for the needs of arms control. Dual-capable systems make it difficult to distinguish between nuclear and non-nuclear systems and even harder to separate the capabilities after systems have been deployed. The simple answer would be to scrap the whole system, but that is not plausible. Vertical launch systems are not even observable, except for cover hatches, so visual identification is ruled out altogether. This situation is in stark contrast to the tremendous US efforts made in the late 1970s to design the MX missile race track system so that it would be readily verifiable by satellite observation. Furthermore, the high degree of automation in a system like the US VLS brings increased risks of inadvertent missile launches, which is not a desirable trend.[87]

Measures

One of the most obvious questions concerning arms control of naval nuclear forces concerns what sort of measures could be envisioned or endeavoured. The possibilities range from limitations on numbers or types of system to their complete elimination. There are, in addition, numerous opportunities for actions that could be considered in the category of confidence-building measures, whether multilateral, bilateral or unilateral. Any attempt to limit, reduce or eliminate naval nuclear weapons would best begin with a political decision on what outcome is desired and what is acceptable. This should be informed by decisions as to the political and military utility of the weapons, whether non-nuclear weapons can substitute for them, whether the change envisioned would cause some undesirable consequence or reaction, and so on.

There are certain types or classes of weapon that could be singled out as having a particular characteristic mandating control, including dubious military value (e.g., nuclear ASW weapons), great pressures to react quickly in a crisis (e.g., ASMs and SAMs), the risk of inflicting serious damage on one's own forces (e.g., SAMs and ASW weapons), or the possibility of having a non-nuclear-armed dual-capable system being presumed to be nuclear (e.g., SLCMs).

On the register of possible confidence-building measures, one could envision actions, such as, publicly declaring which vessels or classes were not nuclear-capable, or, such as, changing the 'neither confirm nor deny' policy and being able to respect the policies of other nations.

Finally, there is the possibility of unilateral measures. It is conceivable that certain measures could be taken which would move towards less nuclearized navies, either reciprocal or not. Although such suggestions have been considered anathema in arms control, it is already the practice of all nuclear weapon powers. All nuclear weapon states decide their own nuclear programmes unilaterally and also the weapon retirement plans. Although NATO may seem to be an exception to this rule, its nuclear weapons are US weapons, and the US ultimately makes decisions (in consultation with its allies) about those weapons. NATO reduced its nuclear stockpile by 1000 weapons in 1980 and is in the process of reducing the weapons based in Europe from roughly 6000 to some 3600, all unilaterally. When older weapons are replaced by newer ones, nations do not negotiate the terms with their adversaries, unless a nation chooses to enter negotiations to extract some price from an adversary for an action that is inevitable and was made unilaterally.

Conclusion

Military 'requirements' drive the positions of arms control negotiators and war planners alike, even though decisions and policies are supposed to come from political authorities. Increasing the political control over both processes would likely open them to more accountability and scrutiny, perhaps with less secrecy and more public debate. It might also introduce more concerns for the questions of arms control and security impact, most of which have been ignored to date.

If the US maritime strategy is entirely for a conventional war, why then does the navy not get rid of its competing and unnecessary nuclear weapons? If the answer is 'deterrence', one must ask what deterrent purpose nuclear ASW weapons serve, or what are the 'unique capabilities' to which Secretary Weinberger euphemistically referred,[88] or why the navy is trying to 'revitalize' its entire non-strategic nuclear weapon forces. These and other questions will not be addressed or answered without some outside stimulation.

If the nuclear weapon nations and navies do not believe that nuclear weapons are necessary for naval warfare and that there are no incentives for any navy to use them, then it is doubtful whether such weapons have any justification. If, however, *any* nuclear navy considers nuclear weapons usable or essential for naval combat, then the danger of nuclear war starting at sea is real and needs to be reduced. These most basic and unanswered questions suggest that naval nuclear weapons have never been fundamentally or critically questioned even within the nuclear bureaucracies or navies, and that there are sound reasons for trying to reduce greatly or to eliminate such weapons. The nuclear navies should explain fully their case for non-strategic nuclear weapons and open these questions to debate.

Notes and references

1　There have only been a handful of articles published in the last 10 years which discuss tactical naval nuclear weapons. There seem to have been even fewer articles that discuss the arms control implications of widespread naval nuclearization. See the bibliography at the end of this study for references.

2　This is exemplified by the United Nations study on *The Naval Arms Race*, A/40/535, UN Study Series no. 16 (United Nations: New York, 1986), by such decisions as the policy of New Zealand prohibiting nuclear-armed or nuclear-powered foreign ships from calling at its ports and by the Greenpeace campaign for 'Nuclear Free Seas'.

3　See, e.g., Norris, R. S., 'Counterforce at sea: the Trident II missile', *Arms Control Today*, Sep. 1985, pp. 5-10; and Slocombe, W., 'Why we need counterforce at sea', *Arms Control Today*, Sep. 1985, pp. 10-12.

4　This trend is well demonstrated in Brooks, L. F. (Captain, US Navy), 'Tactical nuclear weapons: the forgotten facet of naval warfare', US Naval Institute *Proceedings*, Jan. 1980, pp. 28-33.

5　US Department of Defense (DoD), *Report of the Secretary of Defense to the Congress on the FY 1987 Budget* (US Government Printing Office: Washington, DC, 1986) (this annual report will hereinafter be cited as DoD, FY 1987), p. 228.

6　US Joint Chiefs of Staff, *United States Military Posture FY 1988* (US Government Printing Office: Washington, DC, 1987) (this annual posture statement is cited hereinafter as JCS, FY 1988), p. 49.

7　Arkin, W. M., Burrows, A., Fieldhouse, R. and Sands, J. I., 'Nuclearization of the Oceans', background paper for the Symposium on the Denuclearization of the Oceans, Norrtälje, Sweden, May 1984, p. 48; JCS, FY 1979 (see note 6), p. 28, cited in.

8　Cochran, T. B., Arkin, W. M. and Norris, R. S., 'US-USSR Strategic Offensive Nuclear Forces 1946-1986', *Nuclear Weapons Databook*, Working Paper 87-1, Natural Resources Defense Council, July 1987, pp. 5-68; and Meyer, S. M., 'Soviet nuclear operations', *Managing Nuclear Operations*, ed. A. B. Carter, J. D. Steinbruner and C. A. Zraket (Brookings Institution: Washington, DC, 1987), p. 494.

9　US Department of Defense, *Soviet Military Power 1987* (US Government Printing Office: Washington, DC, 1987) (this annual report will be cited hereinafter as *SMP 1987*), p. 43. These Golf II Class submarines are *not* considered strategic weapon systems by the US Department of Defense, since they are deployed in theatres where they have no capability to attack the USA.

10　*SMP 1987* (note 9), p. 31.

11　*SMP 1988* (see note 9), p. 48.

12　JCS, FY 1988 (note 6), p. 37.

13 See Arkin, W. M., 'Sleight of hand with Trident II', *Bulletin of the Atomic Scientists*, Dec. 1984, pp. 5-6.

14 Cochran, T. B., Arkin, W. M. and Hoenig, M. M., *Nuclear Weapons Databook Volume 1: U.S. Nuclear Forces and Capabilities* (Ballinger: Cambridge, MA, 1984), p. 146.

15 DoD, FY 1988 (see note 5), p. 168.

16 For the text of the agreement, see the arms control excerpts of the joint US-Soviet summit statement of 10 Dec. 1987, *Arms Control Today*, Jan./Feb. 1988, p. 16.

17 *World Armaments and Disarmament: SIPRI Yearbook 1986* (Oxford University Press: Oxford, 1986), p. 61.

18 *SIPRI Yearbook 1986* (note 17), pp. 61-3.

19 *SIPRI Yearbook 1987: World Armaments and Disarmament* (Oxford University Press: Oxford, 1987), pp. 33-4.

20 *SIPRI Yearbook 1986* (note 17), p. 61.

21 *SIPRI Yearbook 1987* (note 19), p. 36.

22 *SIPRI Yearbook 1986* (see note 20).

23 DoD, FY 1988 (see note 5), p. 169.

24 DoD, FY 1988 (see note 5), pp. 178-9.

25 *SMP 1987* (note 9), p. 43.

26 See McCormick, G. H. and Miller, M. E., 'American seapower at risk: nuclear weapons in Soviet naval planning', *ORBIS*, Summer 1981, pp. 351-67.

27 JCS, FY 1989 (see note 6), p. 40.

28 Huitfeldt, T., 'Soviet SS-N-21 equipped Yankee in Norwegian Sea', *Jane's Defence Weekly*, 16 Jan. 1988, pp. 44-5.

29 *SMP 1987* (note 9), p. 38.

30 See *SIPRI Yearbook 1987* (note 19), pp. 20-1.

31 See Arkin, W. M., *The Nuclear Arms Race at Sea*, Neptune Papers No. 1, Greenpeace and the Institute for Policy Studies, Washington, DC (Oct. 1987), p. 37.

32 *SMP 1985* (see note 9), p. 103.

33 *SMP 1985* (see note 9), p. 92.

34 DoD, FY 1987 (note 5), p. 228.

35 Table for the 'Nuclear notebook' section of the *Bulletin of the Atomic Scientists*, Sep. 1987, p. 63.

36 *SIPRI Yearbook 1987* (note 19), pp. 20-1.

37 JCS, FY 1989 (see note 6), p. 54.

38 Handler, J. and Arkin, W. M., *Nuclear Warships and Naval Nuclear Weapons: A Complete Inventory*, Neptune Paper No. 2, Greenpeace and the Institute for Policy Studies, Washington, DC, 1988.

39 See Collins, J. M., *US-Soviet Military Balance 1980-1985* (Pergamon-Brassey's: Washington, DC, 1985), pp. 80 and 197. In April 1988 the Danish Minister of Defence included mines in a list of Soviet naval weapons thought to be nuclear-capable. Danish Defence Minister's answer to Question No. S889 submitted by Member of Parliament Jørgen Tved on 15 April 1988.

40 Department of the Navy statement to the US House of Representatives, Committee on Appropriations, Subcommittee on Energy and Water Development, in US Congress, *Energy and Water Development Appropriations for 1986*, Hearings, House Appropriations Committee, 99th Congress, 1st Session (hereinafter cited as HAC, EWDA 1986), Part 7, p. 407.

41 For a history and chronology of nuclear weapons at sea, see Arkin *et al.* (note 7); also in *The Denuclearisation of the Oceans*, ed. R. Byers (Croom Helm: London, 1986).

42 SLCMs present possibilities and complexities that require considerable planning (having the choice of conventional or nuclear warheads, anti-ship or land-attack missions, withholding them as nuclear reserve forces for protracted warfighting schemes, etc.); and nuclear depth bombs are central to US global ASW plans and capabilities. See Brooks (note 4), pp. 28-33.

43 Morrison, D. M., 'The navy's vanishing nuclear arsenal', *National Journal*, vol. 18 (13 Sep. 1986), pp. 2184-5; and Collins, J. M., *US-Soviet Military Balance 1980-1985* (Pergamon: Washington, DC, 1985), chapter 9, 'Naval tactical nuclear trends', pp. 78-85.

44 US Navy, *Nuclear Warfare Operations*, Naval Warfare Publication 28, Revision D, Nov. 1980 (partially declassified) (hereinafter referred to as NWP 28-Rev. D), p. 1-3.

45 HAC, EWDA 1986, Part 7 (note 40), p. 412.

46 US Congress, Senate Armed Services Committee, *Strategic Force Modernization Programs*, Hearings, 97th Congress, 1st Session (US Government Printing Office: Washington, DC, 1981), p. 203.

47 HAC, EWDA 1986, Part 7 (note 40), p. 409.

48 US Congress, Senate Armed Services Committee (SASC), Department of Defense Authorization for Appropriations, FY 1984, DoD, Part 6, Hearings (hereinafter referred to as SASC, FY 1984 DoD, Part 6), p. 3211.

49 US Congress, House Appropriations Committee, Department of Defense Appropriations FY 1980, Part 3, Hearings (hereinafter referred to as HAC, FY 1980 DoD, Part 3), p. 755.

50 Statement of Commodore Roger Bacon to Senate Armed Services Committee, 13 Mar. 1984.

51 HAC, EWDA 1986, Part 7 (note 40), p. 409.

52 JCS, FY 1987 (note 6), p. 35 .

53 NWP 28-Rev. D (see note 44), p. 1-3.

54 Handler and Arkin (note 38), pp. 8-9.

55 HAC, EWDA 1986, Part 7 (note 40), p. 411.

56 Gelb, L. H., 'US contingency plan would put A-arms in four Atlantic nations', *New York Times*, 13 Feb. 1985, p. A-1; Gordon, M. R., 'Whoever called nuclear option just a plan...may not have seen Kissinger's memo', *National Journal*, 6 May 1985, pp. 758-9.

57 Cochran, Arkin and Hoenig (note 14), p. 247.

58 See Arkin, W. M. and Fieldhouse, R. W., *Nuclear Battlefields: Global Links in the Arms Race* (Cambridge, MA: Ballinger, 1985), pp. 62 and 146.

59 See Morrison (note 43).

60 DoD, FY 1987 (note 5), p. 228 .

61 DoD, FY 1987 (note 5), p. 185.

62 For example, in the CG-47 Class cruiser VLS will permit 122 missiles compared to 88 with the earlier MK-26 launcher, and the eventual loading option for Iowa Class battleships envisions some 320-400 missiles per ship with VLS. See Cochran, Arkin and Hoenig (note 14), pp. 264-6.

63 *SIPRI Yearbook 1987* (note 19), p. 25.

64 *SIPRI Yearbook 1987* (note 19), pp. 30-1.

65 Prior to the US maritime strategy debate, the few exceptions to this observation were: Blair, B., 'Arms control implications of anti-submarine warfare (ASW) programs', in US House of Representatives, Committee on International Relations, *Evaluation of Fiscal Year 1979 Arms Control Impact Statements: Toward More Informed Congressional Participation in National Security Policymaking* (US Government Printing Office: Washington, DC, 1978), pp. 103-19; Posen, B., 'Inadvertent nuclear war?: Escalation and NATO's northern flank', *International Security*, vol. 7, no. 2 (Fall 1982), pp. 28-54; Arkin *et al.* (note 7); Ball, D., 'Nuclear war at sea', *International Security*, vol. 10, no. 3 (Winter 1985/86); and Byers (see note 41).

66 See note 65; and *Bulletin of the Atomic Scientists*, vol. 43, no. 7 (Sep. 1987), special section on the 'Superpower arms race at sea', pp. 13-43; Arkin (note 31); Daniel, D., 'The Soviet Navy and tactical nuclear war at sea', *Survival*, vol. 29, no. 4 (July/Aug. 1987), pp. 318-35.

67 DoD, FY 1988 (note 5), p. 169.

68 NWP 28-Rev. D (see note 44), p. 1-2.

69 SASC, FY 1984 DoD, Part 5 (see note 48), p. 2454.

70 See Brooks, L. F., 'Nuclear maritime strategy', US Naval Institute *Proceedings*, Apr. 1987, pp. 33-9; Daniel (note 66).

71 Examples include the Gulf of Tonkin incident in the Viet Nam War, the Cuban Missile Crisis and various nuclear alerts. See Sagan, S. D., 'Nuclear alerts and crisis management', *International Security*, vol. 9, no. 4 (Spring 1985), pp. 99-141.

72 For an excellent treatment of the possible command and control problems, see Bracken, P., *The Command and Control of Nuclear Forces* (Yale University Press: New Haven, CT, 1983).

73 DoD, FY 1987 (note 5), p. 228.

74 SASC, FY 1982, DoD, Part 7 (see note 48), p. 3897.

75 See Arkin *et al.* (note 7); Posen (note 65); Brooks (note 70); Brooks (note 4); and Ball (note 65).

76 See Brooks (note 70).

77 See MccGwire, M., *Military Objectives in Soviet Foreign Policy* (Brookings Institution: Washington, DC, 1987); and Daniel (note 66).

78 See Watkins, J. (Adm., US Navy), 'The maritime strategy', US Naval Institute *Proceedings* (Jan. 1986), supplement, pp. 3-17; and Daniel (note 66).

79 Former US Secretary of State Al Haig, who was the NATO Supreme Allied Commander, Europe (SACEUR) discussed the plans around 1981.

80 Watkins (note 78), p. 14.

81 See, e.g., Halloran, R., 'New Weinberger directive refines military policy', *New York Times*, 22 Mar. 1983, p. 1, and *Washington Post*, 25 May 1983.

82 Watkins (note 78), p. 7.

83 See Fieldhouse, R., 'US naval strategy and nuclear weapons', in *The Uncertain Course: New Weapons, Strategies and Mind-sets*, ed. C. Jacobsen, SIPRI (Oxford University Press: Oxford, 1987), pp. 167-86; Fieldhouse, R., 'Nuclear weapons at sea', *Bulletin of the Atomic Scientists*, vol. 43, no. 7 (Sep. 1987), pp. 19-23; Watkins (note 78); West F. J., 'The maritime strategy' (seminar comments and discussion) US Naval Institute Professional Seminar Series, US Naval Institute, Annapolis, MD, 29 May 1986; and Brooks (note 70).

84 HAC, EWDA 1986, Part 7 (see note 40), p. 408.

85 Joint Summit Statement of 10 December 1987 (see note 16).

86 See Gordon, M. R., 'US aide offers plan to cut arms at sea', *New York Times*, 6 Apr. 1988.

87 See, Frazier, R. L. (Lt Comm., US Navy), 'The sword of the fleet', US Naval Institute *Proceedings*, Aug. 1986, pp. 102-3.

88 DOD, FY 1987 (note 5), p. 228.

Part III. Towards naval arms control

Chapter 4. Naval forces and arms control: a look to the future

Richard Fieldhouse

I. Introduction

From the present to the future

The first two parts of this study concerned the present: a detailed comparison of the superpower navies and a thorough examination of the naval nuclear arms race. This chapter concerns a topic of the future: naval arms control. Although the term 'arms control' is nearly a forbidden topic to the US Navy, it is possible that some similar form of joint US-Soviet co-operation may be the most intelligent way for the superpower navies to sail into the future in a predictable and rational manner that reduces tension and the chances of conflict. Thus, in considering the future of naval forces it is useful to consider the role that arms control could play.

From the previous sections of this study one can conclude four general points about the present superpower naval arms race:

1. It is an important part of the general US-Soviet military competition known as the arms race. This has not been commonly recognized.

2. It is a special and potentially dangerous competition that is under almost no restraints. It needs to be examined from an arms control perspective because some forms of control, restraint or co-operation could help diminish the dangers of the naval arms race while enhancing superpower security.

3. It is, to a remarkable extent, a nuclear arms race—without any controls in place. Non-strategic naval nuclear weapons may be ideal candidates for reduction or elimination.

4. It is clear that the US Navy is much stronger than the Soviet Navy—it is fundamentally a superior force—and that this trend will continue for the foreseeable future. This fact is essential to any rational debate on naval forces, present and future. It is also significant for any

attempt to control or regulate superpower naval forces and activities in the future—where we now turn our focus.

There is only one certainty about the future of superpower naval forces: change. In mid-1988 it is clear that there are numerous changes taking place in and between the USA and the USSR that portend smaller fleets and the possibility of greater US-Soviet co-operation in military and arms control matters, possibly including naval arms control. A short list of the most important changes that will effect the near-term future of the superpowers' navies includes:

• Economic difficulties are causing some serious changes, perhaps more so for the USSR, but are already forcing a reduction of both navies.
• Naval manpower shortages (partly as a result of economic difficulties) are forcing both navies to plan on smaller forces in the future.
• The USSR has been reducing its shipbuilding rate and the scope and tempo of its naval operations.[1] These reductions may well cause a US reaction and slowdown.
• Soviet proposals concerning naval arms control are having an effect on the security and arms control debate and may draw the USA into the debate.
• US-Soviet relations are going through a period of change which brings increased chances for co-operative measures to improve their individual and mutual security. They have started down a path of co-operative security and arms control efforts that will likely take them towards including naval forces in the process. These efforts include recent and pending arms control and confidence-building agreements, summit meetings between the leaders of the two nations, increased contact and improved working relationships between US and Soviet officials at many levels of government and the military, and an expanded dialogue to improve mutual understanding and security. Plans have been made for meetings between the leaders of the two navies and for exchanges of port visits. Many of these changes would have seemed unthinkable as recently as the early 1980s.

Considering these changes, and the seeming inevitability of smaller future fleets and a different security relationship between the USA and the USSR, it is necessary to consider the role that arms control—very broadly defined—could play in helping to shape the future of the superpower navies.

Why consider naval arms control?

One of the first questions that comes to mind when discussing the control of naval forces and activities is 'Why consider naval arms control?'. It is important to think seriously about regulating the superpower navies, as it is for all the military forces of the superpowers, in order to understand how best to prevent war and secure a stable peace.

It is clear that the naval activities and forces of the superpowers, like their other military forces, present risks and dangers that must be considered as possible candidates for measures of control (including limitation, reduction or elimination, risk reduction or confidence-building, and other forms of co-operation). It is also clear, however, that this area of arms control involves many special difficulties and has been neglected for more than 40 years. Although the difficulties can be used as an excuse to avoid thinking seriously about naval arms control, such procrastination will likely complicate matters in the long run and make it more difficult to improve the prospects for peace and security.

The USA and the USSR have committed themselves frequently and officially to seek controls on the various forms of military competition between them. The goals of such efforts, as laid out in various agreements, treaties and national policies, are to reduce the chances of conflict or war, and the aggressive threat or use of military force in contravention of the United Nations Charter. The long-term objectives for arms control negotiations have been to reduce arms to the lowest possible level, to reduce and eventually eliminate nuclear weapons and to seek a programme of general and complete disarmament. To that end the USA and the USSR have participated in bilateral and multilateral negotiations on a wide array of arms control issues, including nuclear forces, chemical weapons, biological warfare and conventional forces.[2]

Naval forces are part of the general superpower arms race and should be considered for the possibilities of control. However, for many particular reasons the control of naval forces and activities has been avoided since World War II. Consequently, the topic of naval arms control has languished for decades, while other areas of arms control have flourished by comparison. It is therefore important to resume the debate on superpower naval arms control.

This chapter is an initial attempt to summarize the issues and questions of superpower naval arms control, beginning with a broad description of what is meant by the term. After reviewing the possible objectives of such efforts, it outlines the basic approaches that are thought possible or desirable, using some examples. The fourth section

describes the major difficulties that complicate or frustrate efforts towards controlling superpower navies. The chapter concludes with a
discussion of the outlook for naval arms control.

II. What is naval arms control and what are its objectives?

For the purposes of this chapter and for the general debate on naval
arms control issues, it is most useful to use a broad definition of the
term to encompass the whole range of possible approaches and measures. This will simplify thinking about the field as a whole, instead of
as many parts. Indeed, all the different measures included have the
same end objective: to bring military activities and forces under control,
by various means, in order to reduce the dangers, risks and possibilities
of war as much as possible. The goal is to prevent war.

Thus, without seeking to create a proper definition, naval arms control could be construed broadly as comprising those measures and activities that seek to prevent or dissuade war by eliminating or reducing
the sources of danger that stem from the naval forces or activities of
various nations. This is a more comprehensive construction than the
traditional but narrow concept of arms control, and includes everything
from negotiated bilateral, multilateral or regional agreements to unilateral or non-negotiated measures, with or without reciprocity, to various forms of joint co-operation ranging from exchanges of information
and personnel to structured dialogue.

Turning to a more specific, although still distinctly theoretical discussion, naval arms control would include the somewhat traditional efforts to limit or reduce naval equipment (for example, the number, type,
size or armament of naval forces, including ships, submarines, aircraft,
personnel and support infrastructure, such as bases and ports). These
can be considered to be efforts at *structural* arms control, since they aim
to impose structural limitations on naval forces.

It is also possible to place controls on the activities of naval forces,
their operations, exercises, formations, movements, deployment areas,
and so forth. These can be considered *operational* arms control efforts,
since they aim to regulate naval operations.[3] Such measures can merge
with a third type of possible control, the so-called *confidence-building
measures* (CBMs). The most well-known recent CBMs are those of the
Conference on Security and Co-operation in Europe, particularly those
resulting from the Stockholm Conference (also known by its abbrevi-
ated name as the Conference on Disarmament in Europe—CDE).[4]

However, virtually any measure that results in increased confidence, openness or understanding, or that reduces the likelihood of dangerous incidents or armed conflict can be considered a CBM. Thus CBMs are the broadest category of arms control.

As they apply to naval forces, such measures presumably could include prior notification of naval activities (including manoeuvres; amphibious activities; formations and movements); exchanges of information about naval force levels, structures and construction plans; and, perhaps even, restrictions on certain types of activity that are agreed to be undesirably risky or provocative. CBMs could also take the form of such agreements as the Incidents at Sea Agreements,[5] which, although not considered arms control by the navies involved, do provide increased confidence and reduced risk to naval activities.

It is also conceivable that other forms of co-ordination or co-operation between navies in peacetime could lead to tacit agreements or understandings that reduce the likelihood of miscalculation or the incentives for adventurous or provocative behaviour. For example, the planned meetings between the leaders of the US and Soviet Navies and reciprocal port visits are only two examples of ways in which the two navies could reduce tension and learn more about each other. These are CBMs of a more routine nature although their cumulative effect could be most significant, and they could pave the way for more far-reaching agreements.

In addition to these three categories of formal, negotiated and agreed arms control, there are possibilities for less formal, non-negotiated and unilateral measures that are designed to achieve similar ends, although with less force than negotiated, ratified agreements offer. In the field of unilateral measures the possibilities include national decisions or policies to do, or not to do, something in order to improve the military or political situation concerning naval forces. These decisions could be publicized in the hope of bringing a similar or reciprocal action/restraint from another nation, or not. One can imagine a wide variety of theoretical options in the naval area, from national decisions on procurement, force structure or choice of armament, to deployment patterns and policies concerning 'naval diplomacy'.

There have been examples of nations agreeing informally to some form of restraint, such as the nuclear testing moratorium of the early 1960s. Such decisions, however, are too easily reversible or not sufficiently credible (as in the case of nuclear 'no-first-use' pledges) to be effective in and of themselves. Critics have sometimes assailed formal arms control proceedings as little more than a process of nations deciding jointly to do what they each would have otherwise done unilaterally, although extracting a price from the other. On this basis, nations could avoid the trouble of negotiating and simply declare their decisions, as did the North Atlantic Treaty Organization (NATO) concerning the removal of 1000 nuclear warheads from Europe in 1980. The presumed purpose of such decisions would be to avoid increasing tension, to decrease it, or to stop further arms competition. On those rare occasions when nations show such restraint, however, they appear to do so primarily for budgetary, managerial or domestic political reasons rather than to avoid confrontation. But it has been unusual for nations to forgo the option of new military technology or forces, even if unaffordable or of marginal, let alone negative, consequence. None the less, the options and possibilities for unilateral action or restraint have not been exhausted.

III. Possible approaches and examples

The three broad categories of naval arms control already mentioned— structural and operational measures; and CBMs—each have current examples in practice. Some of these examples are outlined below, along with some possible approaches that have been suggested but are not currently in practice. The three approaches are listed separately only to simplify their presentation. Efforts to control naval forces could incorporate some or all of these categories of measures in combination, as the history of naval arms control suggests.

Structural measures

Long before nuclear weapons were developed, naval forces were the 'strategic' forces of the major maritime powers. It follows that between the two World Wars naval arms control was an important part of international peacekeeping efforts, as exemplified by the Washington Naval Treaty (1922) and the London Naval Treaty (1930). Limitations and reductions of naval forces have a long, if mixed, history. Today the basic principle remains the same: limits on forces can curtail the capabilities (and thus possibilities) to wage war and can prevent any one nation from gaining a dangerous preponderance of military force. However, given the nuclear capabilities of the five nuclear navies and the technological advances in the capacity to use force, much has changed since the inter-war period.

Structural controls could focus on many elements of naval power: on the quantitative and qualitative dimensions of naval vessels themselves (ships, submarines and aircraft); on the type and number of weapon systems aboard those vessels; on the number of personnel in active naval service; or on the number, placement and capacity of ports and land-based facilities for those forces. Almost no such structural controls are in force today between the superpowers, except for the limitations on ballistic missile submarines and their missile launchers agreed at the Strategic Arms Limitation Talks (SALT I and II). At the US-Soviet Strategic Arms Reduction Talks (START) negotiations in Geneva, both sides are negotiating considerable reductions of their strategic nuclear forces, including submarines, submarine-launched ballistic missiles (SLBMs) and warheads. An agreement along the lines they have been negotiating could increase the proportion of nuclear weapons carried on strategic submarines, while reducing the number of SLBMs and their warheads currently deployed.

Since nuclear weapons are clearly the most destructive and dangerous of the weapons carried by naval forces, they receive most of the limited attention focused on structural naval arms control. But in the START context this has been purely strategic nuclear arms control that happens to include weapons carried by naval forces; until late 1987 there was nothing else remotely naval about it. At the US-Soviet summit meeting in December 1987 both sides committed themselves to finding a way to limit long-range nuclear-armed sea-launched cruise missiles (SLCMs) as part of the START process. This came about largely at Soviet insistence, because the USSR perceives such missiles as strategic and would not accept a START agreement that put no restrictions on US SLCMs. Both sides are exploring ways to verify such limits, but had made no progress by mid-1988. Ironically, SLCMs— which were not even included in the START negotiations until 1988— are the chief obstacle to realizing a treaty.

Other than the START negotiations, there are no limits on naval forces being discussed or negotiated between the superpowers. However, SLBMs and SLCMs are not the only nuclear weapons carried by the US and Soviet Navies. It would also be possible, as some have suggested, to seek limitation, reduction or elimination of the other nonstrategic naval nuclear weapons. Such controls would obviously be difficult to negotiate and verify, but mostly to the degree that the two nations are not interested in controlling these weapons. Recent negotiations on confidence-building measures, intermediate-range nuclear forces (INF) and chemical weapons have shown that verification possibilities have moved past the simple 'it can't be done' mentality that prevailed into the 1980s. Although it may seem a trite observation, it bears repeating whenever people casually dismiss any possibility of controls: political will does play a critical role in determining what is or is not possible in arms control.

Concerning naval non-strategic nuclear weapons, the options for control range from agreements on preventing the deployment of certain future systems to limits on current systems, or to elimination of some or all such weapons. The goal would depend on whether one is focusing on overall capabilities and the dangers of naval nuclear warfare or on the types of weapon that seem most dangerous. It might also be possible to implement controls on the nuclear weapon practices of the four non-strategic nuclear navies (the USA, the USSR, the UK and France), as described below, although these are more of the operational variety.

One could, for example, imagine attempts to limit or prohibit certain types of nuclear weapon, such as nuclear-armed surface-to-air and air-to-surface missiles, given the risks involved in their deployment. However, most such missiles are dual-capable—that is, capable of using either nuclear or conventional warheads. This dual capability of systems complicates any efforts to place controls on them because it is difficult to distinguish between nuclear and conventional models, which makes verification difficult.

Aside from nuclear weapons, other types of naval forces have been suggested for controls. Theoretically, it would be possible, for example, to try to limit the number, type or size of ships deployed with a navy so as to limit its general naval capability. This was the general approach taken in the Washington and London Naval Treaties of 1922 and 1930, respectively, which established categories of ships and then placed limits on their number, tonnage and on the calibre of their guns. But such approaches today would fail to get past some immediate obstacles, such as the asymmetries between most navies. Given the great differences in importance and function between the US and Soviet Navies, it is not possible for them to agree on equal ceilings on their naval forces. Furthermore, if it is not possible to classify two nation's ships into similar categories, it will be difficult to devise equitable and acceptable limitations. Ships often defy such simple classification since they can have vastly different purposes and capabilities. Modern technology permits naval vessels to possess destructive capabilities out of all proportion to their size; limitations on tonnage or size would not necessarily be of any benefit.

Operational measures

Operational controls on naval forces can cover virtually all types of forces and activity. There are numerous examples of such controls in place, ranging from the Montreux Convention, governing naval activities in the Black Sea, to the agreements on preventing incidents at sea, and to zonal arrangements that prohibit certain activities (e.g., the Treaty of Tlatelolco which prohibits nuclear weapons in Latin America). In addition to the existing controls, numerous regional arrangements have been suggested, including superpower naval disengagement from the Indian Ocean and the Mediterranean Sea.[6] In 1976 the USA and the USSR began discussions and negotiations on the question of military disengagement from the Indian Ocean, but these meetings ended without results.

The concept of operational controls is simple: by placing restraints on naval operations or activities, one can try to reduce the opportunities and incentives for conflict. For example, the idea with the zonal or regional approach is to address a specific set of problems or dangers— existing or potential—within a region in order to minimize the chances for war. In practice, however, agreeing on and implementing operational controls could prove difficult and complex. Suggestions for operational controls inevitably confront the paramount desire of naval forces or nations not to be constrained at all on the seas. In such cases the reasons for and benefits of restraint must be compelling to attract national interest. In the case of the USA, even compelling logic would not necessarily result in any desire for controls.

Operational controls could take many forms, depending on the specific issue being addressed. They, like structural controls, could be unilateral, bilateral or multilateral; negotiated or informal. The challenge is to discern the problems or dangers that might be alleviated with some form of control that might appeal to nations and navies alike. One could take the approach of preventing or minimizing provocative behaviour, such as suddenly sending all a nation's submarines to sea without notice, or flying simulated bombing missions against adversary fleet formations or land targets. Generally, if two nations agree that some form of behaviour or action is unwarranted or unacceptably risky, they can agree to cease such operations. In practice, however, nations appear unwilling to give up some actions that are meant to intimidate adversaries in peacetime.

Confidence-building measures

Most operational controls could have the effect of creating confidence between nations. There are other actions which are intended specifically to build such confidence in peacetime, such as the confidence-building measures negotiated at the Stockholm Conference in 1986. Although the CBMs negotiated at Stockholm apply only to activities that are 'functionally related' to military activities on land in Europe, and not to independent air or naval activities, it has been suggested by the USSR and its allies that the next round of the CDE should include naval CBMs on its agenda.[7] Some ideas have been put forward on the subject, but much work is still needed on what such CBMs should be and how they might work (if any can be agreed) before negotiation could begin.

Possible measures could include such elements as prior notification of naval activities, exchanges of information concerning the activities, agreed limits on amphibious manoeuvres, invitation of observers to certain activities, a multilateral agreement comparable to the existing bilateral Incidents at Sea Agreements, and so on. In addition to exchanging information on activities, it might be desirable to exchange information on naval force structure and deployments, and building and retirement plans for naval vessels. Many more suggestions will likely be made in the future as the issue of naval CBMs receives more thought and attention. There are, however, many obstacles to such CBMs, as there are to any form of naval arms control involving the USA and NATO on one side and the USSR and the Warsaw Treaty Organization (WTO) on the other. NATO fundamentally and principly objects to any inclusion of naval CBMs in the CDE process.

Other, less formal, types of CBM are possible that may be easier to agree upon and to implement than the CDE type just described. These could include any arrangement that provides adversaries with increased opportunities for dialogue, regular exchanges, joint efforts to solve or prevent problems, and so forth. For example, starting in 1987 the USA and the USSR began a series of meetings, visits and other co-operative ventures that have a confidence-building result. These efforts include discussions between the highest defence and military officials, joint study of ways to avoid potentially dangerous military incidents—such as the collision of warships at sea—and plans for meetings between the naval leadership and for exchanges of port visits. Such simple, seemingly small steps can help to improve relations and reduce tensions while directing energies into areas of mutual interest. These measures clearly qualify as CBMs, even if they are not called the same. There may be a crucial role in the future for this kind of tacit CBM in a co-operative process of improving security and reducing the chance of war.

IV. Difficulties with naval arms control

Much of the foregoing discussion has been couched in theoretical terms. This is simply because it has proven quite difficult so far to translate the theoretical arms control possibilities into practice. The inherent difficulties involved defy simple solution, so it is necessary to understand them in order to move forward with the naval arms control debate.

Among the current obstacles to naval arms control involving the two superpower navies, perhaps the greatest is their traditional antipathy towards the topic, particularly so for the USA. This disdain largely results from a general naval axiom to preserve the greatest degree of freedom possible in naval action, and thus the least degree of constraint possible. This is especially important to the US Navy as it is the only truly global navy and is a primary instrument of US military power, unlike its Soviet counterpart. The official US attitude towards naval arms control issues appears to be careful avoidance of the subject, lest it gain some air of legitimacy with any form of attention—even adamant opposition. To concede even the possibility of discussing the issue would be seen by many as the first step on a long road of restraints on the US Navy, with disastrous consequences for the nation, its allies and trade partners. Thus, the possibility of a full debate is stifled.

Other impediments to controlling superpower naval forces appear to be longer-term problems as opposed to the attitudinal wall described above. One of the most difficult sets of problems results from the great differences between the two navies, since they have little in common with the exception of the ocean they use. It is frequently argued that the US and Soviet Navies are so fundamentally different in importance, purpose and design that it is difficult to imagine any scheme of arms control between them that would be useful, desirable, equitable or feasible. Part of the problem is the fact that the US Navy is fundamentally in a different league than all other navies. Since it is unquestionably the most powerful navy in the world, it will not gladly concede any of its pre-eminence in the form of limitations.

Part of the problem is that naval forces operate in a medium that is mostly international in character and few restrictions are considered acceptable on the high seas. Nations and navies ardently promote and preserve their freedoms and rights at sea: freedom of navigation, freedom of transit, the right of innocent passage, and so on. These are such important prerogatives that major maritime powers will be loath to let any form of regulation encroach upon them. But, as other analysts have correctly noted, freedom of the seas is also freedom for nations to project power, to intimidate other nations or to otherwise act in a manner unacceptable to coastal states.

Another problem concerns force structure and the asymmetries in purpose, design and capability among naval forces. Naval forces are remarkably different in many respects, which prevents simple comparison or classification for purposes of creating a system for controlling, limiting, reducing or eliminating them. The asymmetries between the US and Soviet Navies alone make it difficult to imagine how one could devise any agreement to control them. What the USSR might seek to limit is either non-negotiable to the USA (perhaps even to the Soviet Navy), and vice versa.

It is often said that the USSR is a land power and that the USA is, by comparison, a maritime power. Consequently, this reasoning suggests that the USSR needs large land forces and the USA needs large naval forces. The argument is frequently made that since the USA depends heavily on oceans for economic and military security, there can be no limitation of its naval forces or activities. This idea is in sharp contrast to the reality of efforts to try to reduce conventional force levels in Europe, where the Soviets are perceived to have a substantial numerical advantage in ground forces. It is not suggested in the West that since the USSR primarily has a land orientation (for many reasons), there should be no efforts to control or limit its ground forces. Quite the opposite position is held: that since the USSR has such large ground forces, it is essential to reduce them. The same logic should hold true for all superpower military forces. Neither side will concede significant advantage to the other and both are publicly committed to a process of trying to reduce their military forces to the lowest possible level while improving security. Naval forces should logically be included in this overall military picture; it may even be a prerequisite for progress in other arms control efforts.

This raises a fundamental question about naval forces and attempts to control them: can one consider naval forces separately from other military forces, or must they be seen as interdependent parts of larger military systems? This may be the most important single issue for attempts to devise controls on naval forces, for its answer would suggest the best approach to take. This question comes with a host of related questions about the role of naval forces in relation to national objectives and to other military forces. If the traditional approaches to naval arms control fail to move forward, it may be because this question has not been adequately examined or answered. There is a logic to the progression of arms control efforts that suggests the need at some point to integrate all military forces into the calculation of what is the lowest acceptable level that is sufficient and least likely to encourage overarmament or belligerence. It is difficult to imagine that conventional arms control and force reductions in Europe could make great progress if the naval forces of the superpowers are completely ignored.

V. Outlook

Although it is impossible and premature to attempt a detailed analysis of the outlook for naval arms control, especially in a chapter of this scope and length, there are several points that can be made.

In the near term the prospects for any formal superpower naval arms control are virtually nil. As long as the USA simply refuses to recognize the topic and even to state or defend its policies and positions, there is simply no hope of the USA discussing or agreeing to any measure outside the possible START reductions of strategic submarines, SLBMs and warheads, and possibly an informal agreement on limiting SLCMs. As of mid-1988, the US Navy had not begun to participate in the public debate on naval arms control, although it now appears to have taken an interest.

Generally speaking, the prospects for formal, negotiated measures of limitation or reduction must be considered quite dim because of the difficulties mentioned earlier. The US and Soviet Navies do not want to give up any of the flexibility or freedom that they so cherish and that seem antithetical to the very idea of controls. According to the US Navy view, naval arms control is a danger. Not only would it not serve any US interest, it would be inherently disadvantageous to the USA and would prevent it from meeting its minimum security obligations. In short, this view suggests that naval arms control could only decrease US security.

The USA currently claims that there is no need for any form of naval controls: there is no danger posed by the superpower naval situation as the US-Soviet Incidents at Sea Agreement and subsequent annual review meetings took care of what few risks once existed and shows that the two navies behave in a responsible and stable manner. Whether this is a sincere position or self-serving protectionism is unclear since the US Navy does not go into any details. It is interesting to note that at their meeting in July 1988 Admiral Crowe and Marshal Akhromeyev agreed to joint US-Soviet efforts to prevent dangerous incidents between their armed forces, including ship collisions like those occurring earlier in the year.

The Soviet Government has, since 1986, increased its public proposals for naval arms control, restraints and CBMs, exemplified by its position at the Stockholm Conference and speeches made by General Secretary Gorbachev. In 1988 Soviet officials—notably Marshal Sergey Akhromeyev, Chief of the General Staff—called for naval forces to be included in European arms control and confidence-building efforts. Although they have provided some new ideas for consideration, these calls for greater restraint and decreased militarization at sea have lacked some of the necessary ingredients of negotiable proposals: necessity, equitability, verifiability and any indication of why the West should take any interest in such controls. Consequently, the proposals have been received with mixed reviews. Some critics in the USA are calling this activity a 'peace offensive' designed to cripple the US Navy. Others see some promise in the direction indicated by the proposals while noting their inherent shortcomings or lopsidedness. But since the USA considers such proposals to be inimical to its interests they are unlikely to be tested by the USA—their intended recipient.

As the single exception to the general situation, there may be good possibilities for the sort of explicit and tacit CBMs that both superpowers are already undertaking: increased contacts and dialogue, risk reduction measures, improved direct communications facilities and procedures, joint efforts to prevent incidents, exchanges of port visits and personnel, and so forth. These sorts of measures are most likely to be accepted and expanded precisely because they are perceived to be clearly in the interest of both nations but do not look like arms control. They could lead the way for more opportunities for using arms control constructively to shape the future of US and Soviet security—and their naval forces and activities. The pressures for change listed at the beginning of this chapter are moving the two nations in this direction; the tide is turning.

It is important to note that the debate on naval forces and arms control is widening and coming closer to centre stage as naval activities come to be seen as increasingly important to issues of peace and security. There is a growing interest in and awareness of naval forces and the unrestrained nature of naval activity, especially the nuclear weapons situation. Many nations besides the superpowers have expressed their maritime security concerns and consequent interest in the topic of naval arms control.[8] If this interest continues, the issue is not going to go away, regardless of how the superpowers act.

If the superpowers wish to pursue a course of arms control and reductions for their security then they must logically include naval forces and activities at some point in that process. Although navies can sail unrestricted on the high seas, they cannot forever be excluded from the general process of controlling and reducing military forces. Naval forces are important elements of military power; in this respect they are no different than ground and air forces. To exclude them from arms control would be a sure means of preventing arms control from moving forward to an important and meaningful point.

It is clear that the objective of naval arms control should not merely be parity or some theoretical balance of naval forces. It is simply artificial to try to impose similar naval forces on nations as different as the USA and the USSR. The objective should be to prevent war, preserve peace and improve security. Otherwise no nations will be interested in the controls. Perhaps only an integrated arms control approach will be able to overcome the complexities and differences of superpower naval forces. Even so, it will not be smooth sailing.

Notes and references

1   See statement of Rear Admiral William O. Studeman, Director of Naval Intelligence, before the House Armed Services Committee, US Congress, 1 Mar. 1988.

2   For an excellent survey of the field, see Goldblat, J., *Agreements for Arms Control: A Critical Survey*, SIPRI (Taylor and Francis: London, 1980).

3   The terms 'structural' and 'operational' are borrowed from R. E. Darilek's analysis of conventional arms control in Europe. See *SIPRI Yearbook 1987, World Armaments and Disarmament* (Oxford University Press: Oxford, 1987), pp. 339-54.

4   For an analysis and the text of the Document of the Stockholm Conference, see *SIPRI Yearbook 1987* (note 3), pp. 339-69.

5   For the text of the agreements, see *Security at Sea: Naval Forces and Arms Control*, ed. R. Fieldhouse, SIPRI (Oxford University Press: Oxford, 1989, forthcoming). There are two bilateral agreements on preventing incidents at sea between naval forces—one US-Soviet and one UK-Soviet. France is also reportedly negotiating a similar agreement with the USSR.

6   See, for example, Blechman, B. M., *The Control of Naval Armaments: Prospects and Possibilities* (Brookings Institution: Washington, DC, 1975); and Cottrell, A. J., and Hahn, W. F., *Naval Race or Arms Control in the Indian Ocean? (Some Problems in Negotiating Naval Limitations)* (National Strategy Information Center: New York, 1978).

7   One of the major concessions at Stockholm that permitted an agreement was the Soviet agreement not to include independent naval and air activities in the final document, but with a promise to pursue them subsequently.

8   This is reflected in the various resolutions, studies and activities of the United Nations, including the study on the naval arms race, responses to that study, and activities at the third UN special session on disarmament in 1988.

Selected bibliography

This bibliography is organized in three sections: general reference works on naval issues relevant to this monograph; sources specifically concerning naval nuclear weapons and warfare; and a short selection of references on the US maritime strategy. Additional references may be found in the notes and references at the end of each chapter.

I. Basic reference works

The United States Naval Institute publishes a monthly journal entitled *Proceedings*. It is the best journal for following developments in US naval thinking, weapons developments, etc.

Arkin, W. M. and Fieldhouse, R. W., *Nuclear Battlefields: Global Links in the Arms Race*, an Institute for Policy Studies book (Ballinger: Cambridge, 1985).

Cochran, T., Arkin, W. and Hoenig, M., *Nuclear Weapons Databook: Volume 1, US Nuclear Forces and Capabilities* (Ballinger: Cambridge, 1984).

Cochran, T., Arkin, W. and Norris, R., *The Bomb Book: The Nuclear Arms Race in Facts and Figures* (Natural Resources Defense Council: Washington, DC, 1987).

Cochran, T., Arkin, W. and Sands, J., *Nuclear Weapons Databook: Volume 4, Soviet Nuclear Weapons* (Ballinger: Cambridge, forthcoming).

Jane's Fighting Ships 1988-89, ed. Capt. R. Sharpe, RN (Jane's Publishing Company Limited: London, 1988), annual volume.

Office of the Chief of Naval Operations, USN, *Understanding Soviet Naval Developments* (5th edn), (US Government Printing Office: Washington, DC, 1985).

Polmar, N., *Guide to the Soviet Navy*, 4th edn (Arms and Armour Press: London, 1986).

Polmar, N., *The Ships and Aircraft of the U.S. Fleet* (13th edn) (US Naval Institute Press: Annapolis, MD, 1984), published about every three years.

Rohwer, J., 'Superpower confrontation on the seas: naval development and strategy since 1945', *The Washington Papers*, vol. 3, no. 26 (Sage Publications: Beverly Hills, CA, and London, 1975).

The Organization of the Joint Chiefs of Staff, *United States Military Posture for FY 1989* (US Government Printing Office: Washington, DC, 1988), annual volume.

United Nations, *The Naval Arms Race*, UN Study Series 16, Document No. A/40/535, United Nations, New York, 1986.

US Congress, House Appropriations Committee (HAC), Hearings on Department of Defense (DoD) Appropriations for FY 1988 (US Government Printing Office: Washington, DC, 1987), annual volume.

US Congress, House Armed Services Committee (HASC), Hearings on Department of Defense (DoD) Authorizations for FY 1988 (US Government Printing Office: Washington, DC, 1987), annual volume.

US Congress, Senate Appropriations Committee (SAC), Hearings on Department of Defense (DoD) Appropriations for FY 1988 (US Government Printing Office: Washington, DC, 1987), annual volume.

US Congress, Senate Armed Services Committee (SASC), Hearings on Department of Defense (DoD) Authorizations for FY 1988 (US Government Printing Office: Washington, DC, 1987), annual volume.

US Department of Defense, *Annual Report to Congress Fiscal Year 1989* (US Government Printing Office: Washington, DC, 1988), annual volume.

US Department of Defense, *Soviet Military Power 1988* (US Government Printing Office: Washington, DC, 1988), annual volume.

II. Naval nuclear weapons and warfare

Arkin, W. M., 'Nuclear weapons at sea', *Bulletin of the Atomic Scientists* (Oct. 1983), pp. 6-7.

Arkin, W. M., Burrows, A., Fieldhouse, R. and Sands, J. I., 'Nuclearization of the oceans', background paper presented to the Symposium on the Denuclearisation of the Oceans, Norrtälje, Sweden, May 1984 (unpublished); much of the paper is published in Byers (see below).

Arkin, W. M., *The Nuclear Arms Race at Sea*, Neptune Papers No. 1, Greenpeace and the Institute for Policy Studies, Washington, DC, Oct. 1987.

Ball, D., 'Nuclear war at sea', *International Security*, vol. 10, no. 3 (Winter 1985/86), pp. 3-31.

Brady, D., 'Nuclear torpedoes' (Comment and Discussion), *Proceedings* (Apr. 1987), pp. 19-21.

Brooks, L. F., Capt., USN, and Miller F. C., 'Nuclear weapons at sea', *Proceedings* (Aug. 1988), pp. 41-5.

Brooks, L. F., Capt., USN, '"New" as in nuclear land attack Tomahawk', *Proceedings* (Apr. 1985), pp. 127-8.

Brooks, L. F., Capt., USN, 'Tactical nuclear weapons: the forgotten facet of naval warfare', *Proceedings* (Jan. 1980), pp. 28-33.

Brooks, L. F., Capt., USN, 'The *nuclear* maritime strategy', *Proceedings* (Apr. 1987), pp. 34-39.

Brown, P., 'Blue-out and nuclear sea states', *Proceedings* (Jan. 1986), pp. 104-6.

Byers, R. B. (ed.), *The Denuclearisation of the Oceans* (Croom Helm: London, 1986).

Caldwell, Jr, H. A., 'Nuclear war at sea', *Proceedings* (Feb. 1988), pp. 60-3.

Center for Defense Information, 'First strike weapons at sea: the Trident II and the sea-launched cruise missile', *Defense Monitor*, vol. 16, no. 6, 1987.

Collins, J. M., 'Naval tactical nuclear trends', *US-Soviet Military Balance 1980-1985* (Pergamon-Brassey's: Washington, DC, 1985), pp. 78-85 and 195-9.

Daniel, D. C. F., 'The Soviet Navy and tactical nuclear war at sea', *Survival*, vol. 29, no. 4 (July/Aug. 1987), pp. 318-35.

Douglass, J. D. and Hoeber, A. M., 'The role of the U.S. surface navy in nuclear war', *Proceedings* (Jan. 1982), pp. 58-63.

Fieldhouse, R. W., 'US Naval strategy and nuclear weapons', *The Uncertain Course: New Weapons, Strategies and Mind-Sets*, ed. C. G. Jacobsen, SIPRI (Oxford University Press: Oxford, 1987), pp. 167-86.

Fieldhouse, R., 'Nuclear weapons at sea', *Bulletin of the Atomic Scientists*, vol. 37, no. 7 (Sep. 1987), pp. 19-23, part of a special section on the 'Superpower arms race at sea', pp. 13-43.

George, J. L., 'I(N)NF', *Proceedings* (June 1987), pp. 35-9. Greenpeace, UK, 'The UK's involvement in the naval nuclear arms race', Greenpeace, London, 1987.

Grove, E., 'Nuclear weapons in surface navies—more trouble than they are worth?', *Defense Analysis*, vol. 1, no. 2, pp. 135-6.

Handler, J. and Arkin, W. M., *Nuclear Warships and Naval Nuclear Weapons: A Complete Inventory*, Neptune Papers No. 2, Greenpeace and the Institute for Policy Studies, Washington, DC, May 1988.

Jordan, J., 'The maritime strategy: the next step' (Comment and Discussion), *Proceedings* (Mar. 1987), pp. 14-16.

Lautenschläger, K., 'Technology and the evolution of naval warfare', *International Security*, vol. 8, no. 2 (Fall 1983), pp. 3-49, esp. pp. 34-8, on 'nuclear weapons'.

Leggett, J., 'The next (nuclear) war happens at sea', *New Statesman*, vol. 114 (6 Nov. 1987), pp. 10-14.

McCormick, G. H. and Miller, M. E., 'American seapower at risk: nuclear weapons in Soviet naval planning', *Orbis* (Summer 1981), pp. 351-67.

Morrison, D. M., 'The navy's vanishing nuclear arsenal', *National Journal* (13 Sep. 1986), pp. 2184-5.

O'Rourke, R., 'Nuclear escalation, strategic anti-submarine warfare, and the navy's forward maritime strategy', Congressional Research Service, US Library of Congress, Report No. 87-138 F, 27 Feb. 1987 (includes excellent bibliography).

O'Rourke, R., 'Nuclear-powered and nuclear-weapon-capable ships in the US Navy: an aid to identification', Congressional Research Service, US Library of Congress, Report No. 86-659 F, 16 Apr. 1986.

Orchard, C. L., 'The Soviet Navy: nuclear war at sea' (Comment and Discussion), *Proceedings* (Sep. 1986), p. 90.

Paolucci, D. A., 'The development of navy strategic offensive and defensive systems', *Proceedings* (May 1970), pp. 205-23.

Paolucci, D. A. and Patton, J. H., 'Nuclear torpedoes' (Comment and Discussion), *Proceedings* (Nov. 1986), pp. 93-4.

Parker, T. W., 'Theater nuclear war and the US Navy', *Naval War College Review* (Jan.-Feb. 1982), pp. 3-16.

Petrofsky, R. A., 'The development of navy strategic offensive and defensive weapons' (Comment and Discussion), *Proceedings* (Nov. 1970), p. 88.

Pocalyko, M. N., 'The nuclear maritime strategy' (Comment and Discussion), *Proceedings* (Naval Review, May 1987), pp. 14-17.

Polmar, N., 'Nuclear war at sea', *Proceedings* (July 1986), pp. 111-13.

Polmar, N., 'Tactical nuclear weapons', *Proceedings* (July 1983), pp. 125-6.

Posen, B. R., 'Inadvertent nuclear war? Escalation and NATO's northern flank', *International Security*, vol. 7, no. 2 (Fall 1982), pp. 28-54.

Quester, G., 'Maritime issues in avoiding nuclear war', *Armed Forces & Society* (Winter 1987), pp. 189-214.

SIPRI Yearbook 1988: Armaments and Disarmament, Stockholm International Peace Research Institute (Oxford University Press: Oxford, 1988). The annual chapter on 'nuclear weapons' provides an overview of all nuclear weapon developments, including naval.

US Navy, *Nuclear Warfare Operations*, Naval Warfare Publication 28, Revision D, Change 1, Nov. 1980 (secret, partially declassified).

Zimm, A., Lt Cmdr, USN, 'The first salvo', *US Naval Institute Proceedings* (Feb. 1985), pp. 55-60.

III. The US maritime strategy

Arkin, W. M. and Chappell, D., 'Forward offensive strategy: raising the stakes in the Pacific', *World Policy Journal*, vol. 2, no. 3 (Summer 1985), pp. 481-500.

Brooks, L. F., Capt., USN, 'Naval power and national security: the case for the maritime strategy', *International Security*, vol. 11, no. 2 (Fall 1986), pp. 58-88.

Lehman, J. F., 'The 600-ship navy', *Proceedings* (Special Maritime Strategy Supplement, Jan. 1986), pp. 30-40.

Mearsheimer, J. J., 'A strategic misstep: the maritime strategy and deterrence in Europe', *International Security*, vol. 11, no. 2 (Fall 1986), pp. 3-57.

Mustin, H. C., Vice Adm., USN, 'The role of the navy and marines in the Norwegian Sea', *Naval War College Review* (Mar./Apr. 1986), pp. 21-5.

The 600-Ship Navy and the Maritime Strategy, Hearings before the Seapower and Strategic and Critical Materials Subcommittee of the Committee on Armed Services, US House of Representatives, 99th Congress (HASC No. 99-33) (US Government Printing Office: Washington, DC, 1986).

Watkins, J. D., Adm., USN, 'The maritime strategy', *Proceedings* (Special Maritime Strategy Supplement, Jan. 1986), pp. 4-17.

For a thorough bibliography on the maritime strategy, see Swartz, P. M., 'Contemporary U.S. naval strategy: a bibliography', *Proceedings* (Special Maritime Strategy Supplement, Jan. 1986), pp. 41-7; and Swartz, P. M., 'Addendum to contemporary U.S. naval strategy: a bibliography', made available by the US Naval Institute Press, Apr. 1987.

Index

USA: attack 64–6, 67–9, 75;
  ballistic missile 8, 52, 54, 98–100
USSR: attack 50, 55–63, 66–7, 68,
  69, 76; ballistic missile 8, 52, 53–
  4, 94–7
see also under names of classes
SUBROC 50, 59, 65, 69, 73, 126, 127,
  128, 129
Super Etendard 36, 131
surface ships:
  general references
  comparisons of 40–4
  numbers 40, 41, 43, 44, 75, 76
  retirement of 42
  individual countries
  France 40, 41
  UK 40, 41
  USA 40, 41, 43–4
  USSR 40, 41, 42, 43
  see also under types of (e.g. aircraft
    carriers)
SUW-N-1 missile 76, 116
Sverdlov Class cruisers 19–20, 21, 42,
  112
Sweden 110
'Swordfish' torpedo bomber 30

Tango Class submarines 61, 63
Tarawa Class ships 36, 122
Terrier missile 128
Third World 7
Ticonderoga Class cruisers 43, 45, 123
Tirpitz, Admiral 21
Tlatelolco Treaty 163
TN-70 warheads 103
TN-71 warheads 103
TN-75 warheads 103
TN-76 warheads 103
Tomahawk missile 55–6, 59, 67–8, 69,
  73, 122–3, 124, 125, 129, 144
Tonnant 103
torpedo boats 18, 19
torpedoes 50, 66–7, 108, 109, 115, 137
  see also under names of
Toshiba Machinery Co. 66
Toulon 131
Trident missile 54, 97–8, 99, 100, 102
Trident submarine 27, 97, 99
Turkey 17, 40, 41
Typhoon Class submarines 23, 53–4,
  58, 61, 72, 96, 97, 116

U-boats 47, 55, 59, 74

underwater acoustics 67, 70–3
Union of Soviet Socialist Republics:
  Afghanistan and 17, 24
  economic problems 21, 39, 70
  secrecy 10
  technology and 21, 23, 56, 66, 74
United Nations, Charter 157
United States of America:
  Congress 123, 128, 129, 136, 137
  debt 27
  Defense Guidance Document 139
  economic problems 27, 43
  forward strategy 46
  military expenditure 26, 27
  naval strategy 8

Vanguard 102
Veinticinco De Mayo 36, 48
Vertical Launch System 129
Victor Class submarines 58, 59, 60,
  61, 63, 65, 68, 111
Viet Nam War 24, 25
Viking aircraft 75
Virginia Class cruisers 123
VLA (Vertical Launch ASROC) 126
Vladivostok 97
V/STOL aircraft 34
VTOL aircraft 34

W44 warhead 126
W68 warhead 100
W81 warhead 128
W87 warhead 100
Warrington 25
Washington Naval Treaty 160, 162
Washington Post 9
Watkins, Admiral James 139, 140
WE-177 bomb 131
Weinberger, Caspar 26, 88, 107, 108,
  115, 128, 134, 136–7, 147
Whiskey Class submarines 20, 22, 59,
  60, 110
World War I 18, 47, 73
World War II 47, 71, 88

Xia Class submarines 101, 104, 105

Yankee Class submarines 23, 52, 59,
  60, 62, 94, 96, 97, 110, 111

Zara Class cruisers 20
Zulu Class submarines 22, 52, 59, 60
Zumwalt, Admiral E. R. 25